Javed Akhtar was born into a dis  His father, Jan Nisar Akhtar, was a writer, and his mother Safia, also a w College in Bhopal. After graduatin ᵧ ᵤ ᵤ‿ollege in Bhopal, Javed Akhtar eventually made his way to Bombay, where over the years he has been associated with some of the biggest blockbusters in the history of Indian cinema, including films like *Deewar, Sholay, Zanjeer* and *Trishul.* For his scripts and lyrics, Javed Akhtar has won the Filmfare Award no less than eleven times. He has also received four national awards as best lyricist. In 1995, he was honoured with the Padma Shri.

Dr. David Matthews, formerly Senior Lecturer in Urdu and Nepali at the School of Oriental and African Studies (SOAS), London University, was born in London. After gaining a first class degree in Classics, in 1965 he became a lecturer in the phonetics of South Asian languages at SOAS, where he first began to study Hindi and Urdu. For his doctoral research he made a study of the Urdu literature of the Deccan. His translations from Urdu into English include works by Rusva, Anis, Hali, Iqbal, Ibn-e-Insha and Shaukat Siddiqi.

Praise for *Quiver*

Javed Akhtar was born with poetry in his blood.... His strength is in his simple diction and modern outlook... [he] is lucky in having found a translator in David Matthews. He has done a splendid job. What Victor Kiernan did for Faiz, he has done for Akhtar.

Khushwant Singh in *Outlook*

Quiver....is overflowing with deep love, emotion and social indignation.... I have enjoyed [the poems], and was deeply moved by some of them.... The translator has quite obviously done a first-rate job.

Frontline

The translator David Matthews' knowledge of Urdu prosody and his understanding of the complicated meters of the Urdu ghazal are impressive.

The Telegraph

...[Javed's] has always been a voice of reason. He is not an artiste in quest of beauty. He is a post-modern writer in quest of meaning.

Business Standard

While no iconoclast, Javed Akhtar is a provocative and thoughtful post-modern poet.

The Pioneer

Quiver

Poems and Ghazals

Javed Akhtar

Translated from the Urdu
by
David Matthews

HarperCollins *Publishers* India
a joint venture with

New Delhi

HarperCollins *Publishers* **India**
a joint venture with
The India Today Group

First published in Urdu as *Tarkash* in 1995
by Sahir Publications

First published in English in 2001

First paperback edition published in 2003
by HarperCollins *Publishers* India

Sixth impression 2009

ISBN: 978-7223-512-7

HarperCollins *Publishers*
A-53, Sector 57, NOIDA, Uttar Pradesh - 201301, India
77-85 Fulham Palace Road, London W6 8JB, United Kingdom
Hazelton Lanes, 55 Avenue Road, Suite 2900, Toronto, Ontario M5R 3L2
and 1995 Markham Road, Scarborough, Ontario M1B 5M8, Canada
25 Ryde Road, Pymble, Sydney, NSW 2073, Australia
31 View Road, Glenfield, Auckland 10, New Zealand
10 East 53rd Street, New York NY 10022, USA

Printed and bound at
Thomson Press (India) Ltd.

*For my children
Zoya and Farhan*

Contents

About Myself

When people write about themselves, the very first thing they mention is the city they belong to. Which city do I call my own? . . . I was born in Gwalior, reared in Lucknow, grew up in Aligarh, played truant in Bhopal and turned wise in Bombay. So why don't I just go into a small flashback, it will be easier for you to read and for me to write my story.

City: Lucknow. Characters: My maternal grandparents, other relatives and I.

I am eight. My father is in Bombay and mother in her grave. My days are spent playing cricket with my younger brother in the courtyard. A fierce looking tutor comes home every evening. That he is being paid Rs 15 a month is a fact I am reminded of every day. Each morning I get a half-anna and every evening an anna to squander—so there's no scarcity of money. In the mornings I buy coloured sweets from Ramjilal, the neighbourhood grocer, and in the evenings the one anna gets me *chaat* from Bhagwati, the hawker from across the road. Life is a party! School has reopened. I am admitted in class six in a well known school of Lucknow—Calvin Talukadar

1

College. Once upon a time it was only the sons of the aristocracy who could study here but now its gates have been thrown open to mere mortals like me. This is an expensive school. My fees are rupees 17 per month (a fact which is . . . well!) Many of my classmates have wristwatches—they come from wealthy families. They wear beautiful sweaters. One even has a fountain pen. These kids buy eight-anna chocolates during recess (Bhagwati's chaat is not appetising anymore). Just yesterday Rakesh announced that his father was sending him to England to study. And yesterday my grandfather chided me, 'You scoundrel, at least pass your matriculation, you may find a job stamping letters in a post office.' At an age when boys dream of becoming engine drivers, I have decided to become rich when I grow up.

City: Aligarh. Characters: My Aunt, other relatives and I.

My younger brother has been retained in Lucknow with my grandparents. I have been allotted to my aunt who has moved to Aligarh. It's understandable. After all, no single family can bear the burden of two orphans. In front of my aunt's home beyond a sprawling ground is my school. Aged fourteen I am in class nine. In Aligarh winter is for real. The school bell strikes at seven. I am on my way there. Razor sharp wind-chill cuts across my face sniping at my nose and ears. School is another story. Somehow I manage to pass. My uncle had remarked to my teacher the day I was admitted to this school, Minto Circle, 'Be watchful, this lad has more interest in film songs than his studies.' I have so far seen Dilip Kumar's *Uran Khatola* and Raj Kapoor's *Shree 420*. I know a lot of film songs but no one is even allowed to listen to them at home, forget about singing them. So I sing on top of my lungs while returning home from school (Excuse me but the early morning chill on way to school would have permitted warbling of only classical ragas). My school is in the university area. Apart from two or three boys from school, I am friendlier with boys from the university. I enjoy whiling away time at restaurants, quite like the older boys. Often I play truant and the school authorities complain. I get a hiding at home to no avail. Textbooks are not after my heart—if I don't like them, well, I don't like them. But I do read a lot of novels inspite of being reprimanded at home. Whenever there is an Urdu poetry contest at the university, it is I who represents my school and win prizes. All the boys and girls of the university know me (that boys recognise me makes me happy: that girls recognise me makes me happier.) I am fifteen and growing up.

Helped by my friend Beelu I write a letter to a girl for the first time. I encounter the girl the next day at an empty badminton court and bravely hand over the letter. Its the first and last love letter of my life. I've forgotten its contents but I remember the girl. I am leaving Aligarh after my matriculation. My aunt weeps as she bids me farewell, prompting my uncle to say that I was going to Bhopal and not to the front. (It's another matter none of us realised then that in a sense I was going to the front.)

City: Bhopal. Characters: Innumerable benefactors, several friends and I.

En route Aligarh to Bombay my father leaves me at Bhopal, or rather midway. I stay a few days with my stepmother's family but soon have to move out. I study at Saifia College and live off friends whose list if I were to compile I would end up with a telephone directory. I am in BA second year and live with a friend, Ejaaz. He pays the rent, I just stay. Although a student, he earns by giving tuition hence friends have nicknamed him 'Master'. I have quarreled with Master and we are not on talking terms so I don't ask him for money. I simply take it from his trousers hanging on the opposite wall or sometimes he silently leaves behind a rupee or two by my bedside.

It's my fourth year in college and I am in my BA final. I have never paid my fees and no one has ever asked. Perhaps this can happen only in Bhopal.

I have been given a vacant room in the college campus to live. After classes are over I pull over a few benches and lay out my bedding to sleep. Its quite comfortable except for the bugs in the benches. The restaurant where I have my meals on credit has closed down, unable to sustain freebooters any longer. There's a shoe shop in its place. Where will I eat now? I am lonely, ill with a high fever and famished. Two collegemates with whom I am hardly acquainted bring some food for me in a tiffin. Strange fools those two but I'm clever by half. I hide my tears till they leave. I recover from my illness and become friends with them. I am a keen debater in college and have won the Rotary Club Prize for three years running.

I have also won several inter-college debates and have represented Vikram University at the National Youth Festival in Delhi. During college elections two opposing groups want me to speak on their behalf. I am concerned not with election but with elocution—I speak on behalf of both.

I have lost the vacant room in the campus and now live with Mushtaq Singh, who earns even as he learns and is also the president of the College Urdu Society. I am good at Urdu. He is better. I know many couplets. He knows more. I am away from my family. He has no family. He seems to be better than me every which way. For a year our friendship has thrived on food and clothes. He provides for both. He is a true Sikh yet buys my cigarettes for me.

I have begun to drink occasionally. Mushtaq and I sit drinking one night as he tells me tales about the Partition and its horrors. Although he was very young then, he remembers: In Delhi's Karol Bagh two Muslim girls were thrown into a scalding drum of coal tar and another Muslim . . . I interrupt him, asking whether he was trying to turn me into a Muslim fundamentalist with his horrific tales! Every story of terror has two sides. What about the other point of view?

Mushtaq Singh smiles. What do you want to hear? 'My story' or a general account. Your story, I say. 'We were a family of eleven. Ten of them were hacked in front of my eyes . . . '

Mushtaq remembers a lot of Urdu couplets—I have been staying with him for over a year. I fail to understand one thing. Good guys, whatever their faith, always end up on the gallows. How was he spared? Nowadays he lives in Glasgow. While we were parting I took off his *kada* and have worn it on my wrist ever since. Whenever I think about him he seems right there with these lines on his lips.

'You pride yourself on your failures,
You are yet unaware of my defeats.'

City: Bombay. Characters: The film industry, friends, foes and I.

On 4 October 1964 I alight at the Bombay Central station. This is the court where my fate will be sealed. Within six days of my arrival I have to leave my father's home. I have twenty-seven paise in my pockets. I am happy that if I am able to add another paisa to my riches I will be the winner and life a loser.

It's been two years in Bombay. There's still no certainty of either food or shelter. I have managed to write dialogue for a minor film for Rs 100 per month. Sometimes I work as an assistant, sometimes as an errand boy. Sometimes an odd job comes along; most times even that is hard to find. I go to a film producer's office at Dadar to collect money for some comic scenes I have ghostwritten but which will be credited to a famous screenwriter in the film. The office is shut. I think about the long trudge back to Bandra. I have just enough money to either grab a bite or a bus ride. I buy some *channa* and start walking. Ambling past the gate of Kohinoor Mills I think that things may change but this gate will remain and one day

I will drive past it in my own car. I have got an assignment to write dialogue in another film. I reach the director's home with the scenes. He is having pineapple for breakfast as he reads the scenes. Throwing the papers at my face he dismisses me, saying I would never become a writer. Walking out into the blazing sun I wipe a tiny tear and think that one day I shall show this director that I . . . Suddenly a thought crosses my mind, 'Does this fellow have pineapple for breakfast everyday?'

It is perhaps two in the morning. The Bombay monsoon is at its worst fury. The sea seems to be pouring from the sky. I am sitting under the pale yellow light of a weak lamp on the steps of Khar station's portico. Close by three men sleep on the floor unmindful of the raging storm. In a distant corner a wet dog shivers away. Incessant rain pours on dark empty streets. Lights went out in silent buildings long ago. People must be sleeping in their homes. Somewhere in this city is my father's home. What a large metropolis is Bombay and how small am I . . . insignificant even. However much one clings to courage, there are moments one feels scared . . . very scared.

For a year now I have been living in Kamaal Studio (present-day Natraj Studios). I sleep wherever I fancy— sometimes in a verandah, sometimes in a corridor, sometimes under a tree. There are several homeless, jobless people like me who live here. One of them is Jagdish, who becomes my friend. Everyday he has a new plan to get a free meal and a free drink. In fact, Jagdish has turned survival into an art form.

I have become acquainted with a second-hand bookseller on the pavement outside Andheri station so there's never a shortage of books to read which I do till late into the night in the dim light of the studio compound. Friends often mock me, saying I would soon go blind with all this reading. I get a chance to sleep inside a room. This has the studio wardrobes where costumes of the film *Pakeezah* are stored. The shooting of this film has been suspended as Meena Kumari and Kamaal Amrohi have separated. One night I open one of the wardrobes and amidst assorted shoes and sandals lie the three Filmfare trophies which Meena Kumari has won. I dust them and keep them aside. This is the first time I have touched a film award trophy. Every night I bolt the door and with the trophy in my hands I stand before a mirror imagining the day I would be receiving these awards; amidst all the applause how I would wave to the audience. Before I can perfect my act a notice is put up in the studio prohibiting non-workers from staying in the compound. Jagdish suggests an interim arrangement of shifting to the Mahakali Caves (these ancient Buddhist caves in crowded east Andheri near Kamalistan Studio were part of a desolate landscape in those days where hemp smoking mendicants lay about). The mosquitoes here are monstrous and they wake you up by just sitting on your body. In one night I figure out that to sleep here you need the stupor of hashish. Somehow I pass three days before a friend asks me to stay with him at Bandra. As I leave for Bandra, Jagdish says that he too will find a new abode in a couple of days (This was my last meeting with Jagdish. In the years to come life took me to new heights but for eleven years Jagdish languished in those caves in a haze of pot-smoke and hooch. He was cremated by the sadhus and neighbouring slum-dwellers who pooled together some money. The End. My friends and I learnt of his death much later. I often wonder, what is so special in me that Jagdish lacked? There is always the possibility that a friend of Jagdish's could have invited him to stay at Bandra and I was left behind to perish in those caves. (It all seems so arbitrary. . . Why the vanity then?).

The friend with whom I am living in Bandra is a professional gambler. He and two of his accomplices are card sharps. They teach the tricks to me too. For a few days the cards provide the means of survival but then the three men leave Bombay and I am back to square one—who will pay the room rent for the next month? A famous and successful writer calls and offers me a job at Rs 600 per month. The work is to ghostwrite for him. Six hundred rupees at this point is worth six crores. I contemplate. If I accept I may end up doing the job for the rest of my life. On the other hand there's the rent to pay. Then I think what the hell . . . I reject the offer after three days of thought. Days, months, years roll by. It's been five years in Bombay. 'Roti' is a moon and fate stormclouds. The moon reveals itself on somedays and is elusive on others. These have been five difficult years for me but I have retained my dignity. I am not disillusioned. I have faith. I shall overcome. I am not born to just survive. At last in November 1969 I get some work, which in film parlance is called a 'break'.

Success is like Alladin's magic lamp. Suddenly the world is beautiful and people kind. In a matter of just over a year I have got a lot and more is on its way. I see the dust I touch turn to gold. My first house, my first car. Dreams are coming true but life is still lonely. I meet Honey Irani on the sets of *Seeta Aur Geeta*. Open-hearted and frank, she has a cheerful demeanour. Within four months we are married. I invite a lot of my father's friends to my wedding but leave him out. (Even the genie of Alladin's lamp cannot heal all wounds. It takes time.) In two years we are proud parents of a daughter, Zoya, and a son, Farhan.

The next six years see a string of blockbusters. Awards and acclaim. Fame and fortune. Parties and write-ups. Travel around the world. Bright days and dazzling nights. Life is a technicolour dream but like all dreams this one too shatters. For the first time one of my films flops (there have been several hits and misses since but the joy with its earlier innocence is lost somewhere).

My father dies on 18 August 1976 (Nine days before his death he had given me his last book. He had autographed and inscribed it with these words: 'You will remember me when I am gone.' He was right.) Until then I had thought of myself only as a rebellious and angry son. Who am I now? I look at myself and the world anew and ask myself whether I have got what I wanted from life? Others do not realise it but I am no longer enamoured or content with things which hitherto gave me much joy. I am attracted to things the world considers unprofitable. My relationship with poetry runs deep and my interest in it is inborn. I knew even in my adolescence that I could write poetry but have not done so thus far as a symbol of my angst and rebellion. I write my first poem in 1979 and make peace with both my father and my legacy. During this period I meet Shabana. Kaifi Azmi's daughter is also perhaps retracing her roots. She too is troubled by new questions and doubts. It's not surprising that we come close. I am being metamorphosed. Even my professional partnership ruptures. My friends notice my transformation with concern. Honey and I are separated in 1983.

(Our marriage may have fallen apart but even a divorce does not diminish our friendship. And if our children do not have the bitterness of a broken home it is more to Honey's credit than my doing. Honey is today a successful screenwriter and a good friend and there are but a few in this world for whom I have as much respect as I have for her).

Although I had moved ahead, life could well have become a journey from a hotel room to a hospital bed. I was always a heavy drinker but began drinking even more. This is one phase of my life I am ashamed of and if people tolerated me during this time it was their benevolence. It was quite possible that I could have died during one of my drinking bouts. However, someone's remark one morning touched me so deeply that I have never touched alcohol since and never will.

Today when I look back at life I see a river emerging from the mountains, battling with rocks, meandering through gorges, bubbling and frothing, creating ripples as it flows. Where once it broke its banks the river has now reached the plains. Tranquil with waters running deep. My children, Zoya and Farhan, have grown up and are finding their bearings in the world outside. In their eyes twinkle dreams of tomorrow. Salman, my younger brother, is a successful psychoanalyst in America. He has written several books, is a good poet, and a doting father of two intelligent kids. Life was no easy journey for him either but with hard work and dedication he has reached his destination and beyond. I am happy and so is Shabana who is not just my wife but also my beloved who has a beautiful heart and an invaluable mind. 'The world I'm from, she belongs to that world.' Had my uncle Majaaz not written these lines I would have written them for Shabana.

Today although life has been kind to me in every way I remember one particular day—18 January 1953. Place: Lucknow, my grandparent's home. A weeping aunt takes my six-year-old brother and me to a large room in the house where many women are seated on the floor. I can see the uncovered face of my mother who is lying wrapped in a white shroud. My old grandmother, held gently by two women, sobs silently besides her. My aunt takes us closer to the body and bids us to have a last glimpse of our mother. I had celebrated my eighth birthday just yesterday. I understand. I know what death is. I gaze intently at my mother's face so that I can freeze it in my memory. My aunt is saying, 'Promise her you'll become something, promise her you'll do something in life.' I cannot say a word but just keep staring till someone covers my mother's face with the shroud.

It is not that I have not done anything in life but I have done just a quarter of what I can. This thought makes me restless. Always . . . .

Translated from the original
by Amit Khanna

Introduction

For audiences in India and Pakistan, Javed Akhtar requires no introduction. His films alone have gained him universal recognition, and his lyrics, which have been sung by some of India's most famous vocalists, are known to everyone. Although in his verse he frequently refers to his own shortcomings and ineffectualness, his life has been one of outstanding success. Having graduated from Saifiya College in Bhopal, he eventually made his way to Bombay, just as many in the Urdu-speaking community of India had done before him. There the growing film industry provided him with the opportunity to exploit his talent for writing to the full.

Before the fall of the last remnants of the Mughal dynasty in 1857, Urdu poets, who could hardly make a living from what they wrote and published, looked to the courts of Delhi, Lucknow and Hyderabad, and to the great houses of the nobles for patronage. When the old order collapsed and aristocratic families were no longer able to afford the luxury of keeping a private group of poets to adorn their courts, aspiring writers were obliged to look elsewhere. Although during the later stages of

British rule, Urdu, once regarded as the language of culture and refinement *par excellence*, suffered a number of setbacks, it still held on to its prestige. The *ghazal*, a form of lyric verse which had its origins in medieval Persia, remained eternally popular, and traditional poetic gatherings, known as *mushairas*, continued to attract, as they still do, audiences of thousands. The story of the broken-hearted lover frustrated in his endeavours to approach his cruel, uncaring mistress, the images of the lonely bulbul singing its heart out in the garden decked with the tulip and the rose, the fervent desire for annihilation and escape from the material world and the dream of attaining union with the creator—all these elements of the *ghazal*, with its elegant Persian diction, were instantly familiar to people of whatever religion, caste or social background. It is, of course, the *ghazal* that people have in mind when they refer to Urdu's 'sweetness'.

In the early decades of the twentieth century, Urdu poets turned their attention in other directions. The growing impatience for independence from the British rule and the fervour of the freedom movement provided many with an outlet for their talents. At that time, for expressing dangerous political views in particular, verse could be even more effective than prose. Many young progressive writers like Javed's father, the eminent poet, Jan Nisar Akhtar, emerged largely from the small towns of Uttar Pradesh, where Urdu had been born and had been cultivated for centuries. These writers used their skill and energy to produce a vigorous modern literature, which played a significant role in carrying the subcontinent along its path to independence. Here the place of poetry cannot be underestimated, and the names of Jan Nisar Akhtar, Kaifi Azmi (Javed Akhtar's father-in-law), Josh Malihabadi, Ali Sardar Jafri, Majruh, Faiz Ahmad Faiz and Javed Akhtar's maternal uncle, Majaz, to name but a few, have become legendary. Many of them spent periods of time in jail for the views and beliefs which were expressed in their writing.

This is a clear indication that their British masters took the power of verse very seriously indeed. Urdu was never the exclusive preserve of one people and many Hindus and Sikhs joined the ranks of its largely Muslim writers, nor was it restricted to only one region of India, but was written and spoken and cultivated in cities as far apart as Delhi, Lahore, Karachi, Bombay, Hyderabad and Calcutta. Even though, largely for political reasons, the language has in recent years suffered a decline, the verse and prose of these early 'progressive' writers is still remembered with a respect which often borders on awe.

When independence was finally achieved and the film industry of Bombay began to grow, talent for providing scripts and for composing songs, which always form an essential part of a Hindi film, was urgently required. It was largely from this well-established group of Urdu writers that it was sought. From the 1950s onwards, perhaps, it would be fair to say that Bombay replaced the Red Fort as the new bastion of Urdu poets.

When writing for films, poets, novelists and musicians at the same time continued with their 'more serious' work, applying all their skills and traditions to the scripts they prepared. For this reason it is often impossible to distinguish between a film lyric and a carefully constructed poem, written according to norms of classical verse. In the West popular songs are not normally written by 'serious' poets, but in India they usually are. In the subcontinent classical poetry is still very much a part of the fabric of everyday life, and many people with no particular literary education—they might be engineers, doctors, taxi-drivers or waiters—can recite scores of verses from memory. In Britain it would be hard to find anyone with such a knowledge of Keats, Byron or Shelley. There, poetry is usually read, if read at all, from books. In India and Pakistan it is recited on the street and in cafés.

This is the milieu into which Javed Akhtar was born. His father, Jan Nisar Akhtar, was already a well-established poet and writer, and his mother, Safia, taught at the Hamidia College in Bhopal. His uncle, Majaz, was highly respected for his verse, and his grandfather, Muztar Khairabadi, holds a distinguished position in the history of Urdu literature. It is not surprising that when we read Javed Akhtar's work, we find many echoes of his forebears.

In his early childhood, Javed Akhtar would have seen many of the great literary figures of the time, and in poetic gatherings, whether held in public or at home, he quickly became familiar with traditional metres and cadences of Urdu verse. Indeed in the subcontinent people do not have to be taught prosody. Induction from the earliest days of childhood makes the flawless construction of verse a natural process. The rhythms of Urdu verse still depend upon a complex and intricate system of

18

prosody developed by the Persians before the tenth century AD. The rules regarding the quantity of long and short syllables are rigid and allow for no deviation or licence. In more recent times, poets have begun to ignore the rules and to write in irregular 'free verse', but even here the traditional cadences can still be detected. In India, it would appear, no matter how hard one might try, the values of the past can never be completely ignored.

After graduating from Bhopal, Javed Akhtar made his way to Bombay. The city offered many opportunities to a young man who wished to pursue a literary career, but there were, as in any life, moments of frustration and despair. His mother, to whom he had been very close, and whom he frequently mentions in his poetry, had died. After his arrival in Bombay at first things did not go well, and apparently without friends and support he often wandered the streets without eating. His feelings, as he roamed the crowded, chaotic bazaars, eventually finding himself almost in a state of collapse lying on one of the ghats, are forcefully expressed in his poem *Hunger*:

> 'I see a pipe, I see a tap,
> But why then is the water hard?
> It seems as if a blow is thrust
> Against my stomach.
> Now I feel that I might faint,
> And sweat engulfs my body.
> I have no strength left.
> Three days today!
> Three days today!'

This poem, incidentally, breaks with tradition by having no rhyme, but still preserves one of the traditional metres of classical Urdu verse.

It was not long before Javed Akhtar found his place in the flourishing literary world of Bombay, which during the 1960s had established itself as one of the great progressive centres for Urdu letters. In many ways, Bombay and Karachi were rapidly overshadowing Delhi and Lucknow, where Urdu had previously been born and nurtured. It was natural that he, like many others, should join the film industry, and with his partner, Salim Khan, he scripted many 'hit' films, including the memorable *Deewar, Sholay, Zanjeer* and *Trishul.* Among the rising actors of the time was Amitabh Bachchan, who in the scripts of Javed and Salim took on the role of the 'Angry Young Man'.

Thereafter, Javed Akhtar's success and popularity with the public never waned. Branching out on his own, he wrote films like *Sagar, Mr. India* and *Betaab,* and for his scripts and lyrics won the Filmfare Award no less than eleven times. He received four National Awards for best lyric writer. Other accolades, too numerous to mention here, followed. In 1995, at the zenith of his career, he received the Padma Shri.

The present volume of Urdu poems, entitled *Tarkash* (Quiver), was first published in 1995, and is now in its fourth edition. After its publication it was immediately translated or rather transliterated into Hindi, being thus assured of an even wider readership. The Hindi version, which is exactly the same as the Urdu original, only presented in a different alphabet, has now reached its eighth edition. Translations have also been made into Bengali and Gujarati, and it has also been released as India's first audio book, available on both cassette and CD. Javed Akhtar has visited the United States to give lectures on his work, and some years ago was invited to London to read his poems before a group of students and teachers in the School of Oriental and African Studies, where Hindi and Urdu are given great prominence. As he recited his verse without a pause, the audience sat spellbound.

No vignette on Javed Akhtar's life would be complete without the mention that he is married to Shabana Azmi, one of India's greatest actresses. It is to her that *Tarkash* is dedicated. Shabana is the daughter of Kaifi Azmi, a contemporary of Jan Nisar Akhtar, who formed part of the group of activist Urdu poets at the time of independence. Kaifi Azmi, always well loved and well respected, even in his later years, can still attract large audiences when he appears in public to recite his work. His daughter Shabana, an actress who is no stranger to controversy, has recently embarked upon a new career as an independent politician.

In describing the poetry of Javed Akhtar, commentators have employed a wide range of complimentary adjectives, which attest to its overall excellence. In her introduction to the Urdu edition of *Tarkash*, the distinguished Urdu writer Quartulain Haidar says: 'Javed Akhtar is an eloquent, thoughtful post-modern poet. Freshness, depth, intellectualism and a search for new meanings in life are the characteristics of his verse . . . sometimes he can write traditional poetry, but never bad poetry.' She makes the further point that 'Tarkash is filled with the arrows of life's sadness and of the grief of the age'.

In Urdu poetry, especially in the ghazal, of which twenty-three examples are found in this anthology, words such as gham (grief), dard (pain), khalish (pricking), aafat (disaster) and tanhai (loneliness) are almost obligatory. The concepts of firaq (separation) and its opposite, the unattainable visal (union with the beloved) have always been part of the tradition. It is, of course, how the poet uses them, and what he or she makes of them, that is important. The loosely strung couplets of the lyric can say different things to different people, and in most cases they defy a single hard and fast explanation or interpretation. Perhaps the reason for the great popularity of Javed Akhtar's verse is that on the surface it appears disarmingly simple and direct, but frequently it has something profound and significant to communicate. It is thoughtful without being pretentious. Javed Akhtar is always capable of putting into words thoughts and ideas which all of us have, but which we are seldom capable of expressing so neatly and so meaningfully ourselves. To illustrate this we can take a few verses at random:

'My house has been surrounded with high buildings;
I have been robbed of my share of the sun today.'

'All of us are just one step from happiness;
In every house we always seem to lack one room.'

'They say that history repeats itself today.
But then the best parts always seem to go astray.'

'Someone robbed my sea of wind
And left me with a sailing boat.'

The familiar story forming the basis of the ghazal, which ultimately goes back to the Arabic tale of the lover, Majnun, who lost his senses in his impossible quest for his beloved, Laila, is succinctly and humorously summed up in just one couplet:

'See! Here is love and union and separation!
So let's go back; there's much work to be done.'

Reminiscences of childhood and early life, which Javed Akhtar spent in the secure and comfortable house of his maternal grandparents in Lucknow, are strong and are found in many poems throughout the book. This was a happy time, free from life's complications and uncertainties. Everyone knows what it is like to return home after a long period of absence and to find the familiar tree still growing in the courtyard of the old house. The room in which the poet used to take refuge, with its heavy door and solid, reliable furniture, is remembered with longing and great affection. There he would sleep securely and sometimes gaze at the ceiling before going to sleep:

'In the rafters of the roof
No one knows how many tales were begun.'

When starving in the streets of Bombay he looks at the full moon, which in accordance with Indian poetic

23

tradition reminds him of a round *chapatti* served up on the dish of the sky. He at once recalls how his mother used to feed him when he was a child and had no cares:

> 'And what strange things my mother said,
> As every day with her own hand
> She used to feed me as she spoke . . .
> "One mouthful for the elephant
> Another mouthful for the horse,
> One more mouthful for the bear." '

Success in life can bring us wealth, and the new house which we move into might be far grander and more magnificent than anything we ever imagined in our childhood. But like the pawn, which progresses form square to square, gradually eliminating all its opponents and even distancing itself from its friends, we acquire this comfort by sacrificing so much of what we formerly cherished:

> 'This is the day when my own people break with me,
> But once the bough would bear my weight so easily.

> This is the day when sleepless nights stare at the wall,
> But once in sleep my heavy eyelids used to fall.

> This is the house with everything on every side;
> That is the house where my grandmother lived and died.'

In Javed Akhtar's verse there is much talk of love, its complications, its pains and even its joys. For the traditional lover the path towards his goal is rarely smooth. Thorns tear his body as he traverses the desert, his feet

24

are blistered, he tugs at his collar in distraction, and cast into chains, he is mercilessly tortured in the flames of oppression. But, for all his suffering, his indifferent mistress hardly notices that he exists:

'The tip of every thorn is reddened with my blood;
The traces of my searching are the desert flowers.'

'It's we who stop and block the street;
We are the blisters on our feet.'

'They're burning me alive, but do not know
My chains are slowly melting in the glow.'

'She does not even know that I exist, as if
She is a sundial; I, a moment of the night.'

The hopeless quest of the poetic lover is, of course, an allegory of all the frustrations we come across in life. It is rare that we attain all that we desire, and finally we become resigned to our lot. Such lines can usually be interpreted in whatever way the reader wishes.

This is the traditional approach to love, which has fuelled romantic Persian and Urdu literature for centuries. But there are sweeter moments, memories of love fulfilled, which are recounted with fond nostalgia:

'We're close, but we are far away.
There was a secret when we met.
She remembers someone still,
And you—I just cannot forget.'

'If I compose a verse
Or read of something new . . .

If I am greeted by a sight
Which is stunning,
Some moment
Which touches my heart—
I store all these things
In the recesses of my mind
And think
That when we meet
I shall tell them all to you.'

There are even times when the goal seems to have been reached, and love finally overcomes all the obstacles that once lay in its path:

'I was very clever then,
And you were very cunning too.
First we thought it was a game.
Now you love me, and I love you.'

In Indian love poetry the description of female beauty has a long tradition. It is found in the earliest Sanskrit texts, and forms an integral part of the Urdu narrative romance. Here the images are taken from familiar Indian scenes, and words are deliberately chosen from Hindi as opposed to Persian or Arabic. In this kind of verse, often composed in native Indian rhythms, we find black eyes highlighted with *surma* or kohl, the distinctive red spot placed on a forehead curved like the crescent moon, dark tresses hanging like poisonous snakes over pale cheeks. Ankle bells tinkle and the perfumed forests become luxuriant under the rains of the first monsoon. In poems of untranslatable beauty, Javed Akhtar captures such scenes, which will be instantly recognisable to his readers:

'Glowing body, painted lips, magic eyes, curly hair; Shining marble, scarlet cloud, red horizon, frightened deer.

Cobra for the charm-pipe, shade for the yard, tinkling bells, hope for the heart,
Eyes with kohl, clouds and hills, your flowing locks, my arms apart.

Perfumed nights, burning breath, drunken eyes, rainy weather,
Dreams of beauty, toys of love, scattering flowers, we together.'

Again, following an old tradition, the *banjara*, the Indian equivalent of the gypsy, who goes restlessly from town to town selling his wares, wanders through Javed Akhtar's cities of dreams, taking his rest upon a mound of loneliness, telling his tiny moments of all that might have been.

It would be wrong, however, to imagine that the *ghazals* of Javed Akhtar are merely simple love poems. They may appear to be so on the surface, but they usually contain a much deeper message. Eventually it is up to the reader, or rather the listener, to explore the various levels for himself or herself. The very vagueness of expression offers countless possibilities, and this poses great problems for the translator, who is often put in the position of trying to read the poet's mind. A translation of a verse can usually offer only one interpretation, although several others may be possible. This difficulty can only be solved by offering a commentary, but exegesis has no place in a work of this kind. I would not presume to give a synopsis of Javed Akhtar's philosophy of life, which we find expressed in his poems, but a number of points clearly emerge. In all societies there are many glaring injustices, and it is our responsibility to recognise them and do all we can to oppose them. We are usually totally ineffectual in doing so, even though we try our best to live up to the standards we have set ourselves. In the end we have to admit that we, like everybody else, are never totally honest, but even so we should have the courage to say so:

'Interesting, but never truthful, you and me!
We seem quite good, but we're not good at all, you see.'

'It may take endless time to reach a distant goal,
But slipping back does not take any time at all.'

Tarkash also contains a number of lengthy philosophical poems, which deal with some of mankind's more profound worries and anxieties. Most of these poems dispense with rhyme and metre, an indication perhaps that they are regarded as more serious works than the delectable love lyrics. Questions are raised, which many people would perhaps be too embarrassed to ask. What is the nature of time and space? What is the reason for the suffering and the abject poverty instantly visible on the streets of any Indian city? If Mother Teresa comforted the poor, why did she not pause to examine the social conditions which made her admirable mission necessary?

After a riot, when shops and buildings lie wrecked and bazaars are looted, should we not spare the time to find out why the looters acted as they did? These questions are asked in a soft, calm voice, which does not preach or pontificate. The poet does not set himself up as the orator, who already knows all the answers. He merely asks simple questions to which the response remains a mystery.

In translating Javed Akhtar's verse into English, I have tried to be as faithful as possible to the text and hope to have captured some of the spirit of the original. No version put into another language, the poetic traditions of which are very different, can do both adequately. It is a truism that perfect translation of verse is virtually impossible. But it can be equally argued that any translation is better than no translation at all. The ghazal, with its complicated metres and rigid rhyme scheme, presents the greatest challenge of all. The pattern of the rhyme AA, BA, CA, . . . does not easily lend itself to English, and cannot be completely imitated without contorting the syntax beyond all reasonable bounds. But much Urdu verse is rhythmical and rhymed, and it is this, among other things, which gives the ghazal its outstanding poetic beauty. Somehow this must be reflected, and blank-verse renderings rob the poem of at least half of its charm. Some compromise must therefore be sought, even if it means putting the lines of the ghazal into rhyming couplets, which constitute part of the English tradition. In most cases, when the original Urdu poem is rhymed and metrical, I have adopted this approach; when the Urdu poem is written without rhyme and metre, I have translated accordingly into blank verse. The reader must, of course, decide how far I have been successful in my translation, but if some of the charm and beauty of Javed Akhtar's poetry has been preserved, then at least something has been accomplished.

David Matthews
London

What have you done in your life? Have you loved someone with a sincere heart? Have you given a friend some good advice? Have you looked at the child of an enemy with love in your eyes? Where there was darkness, have you brought a ray of light? For all the days you have lived, what was the point of this life? . . .

Krishan Chandar

मेरा आँगन, मेरा पेड़

मेरा आँगन
कितना कुशादा[1] कितना बड़ा था
जिसमें
मेरे सारे खेल
समा जाते थे
और आँगन के आगे था वह पेड़
कि जो मुझसे काफ़ी ऊँचा था
लेकिन मुझको इसका यक़ीं था
जब मैं बड़ा हो जाऊँगा
इस पेड़ की फुनगी भी छू लूँगा
बरसों बाद
मैं घर लौटा हूँ
देख रहा हूँ
ये आँगन कितना छोटा है
पेड़ मगर पहले से भी थोड़ा ऊँचा है।

---

[1] फैला हुआ।

My Courtyard, My Tree

My courtyard
How wide it was, how vast!
The yard in which
All my games fitted so well.
And in front of that yard stood that tree,
Which was much taller than I.
But
I was sure
That when I grew up
I would manage to touch the top of that tree.
After so many years
I have come back home
And I see how small
My courtyard really is.
But the tree is even a little taller
Than it was before.

गिन गिन के सिक्के हाथ मेरा खुरदुरा हुआ
जाती रही वो लम्स[1] की नर्मी, बुरा हुआ

---

[1] स्पर्श।

From counting coins my hands grew gnarled—and that was sad.

I lost the softness of my touch—and that was bad.

ग़ज़ल

हमारे शौक़ की ये इन्तहा[1] थी
क़दम रक्खा कि मंज़िल रास्ता थी

बिछड़ के डार से बन-बन फिरा वो
हिरन को अपनी कस्तुरी सज़ा थी

कभी जो ख़्वाब था वो पा लिया है
मगर जो खो गयी वो चीज़ क्या थी

मैं बचपन में खिलौने तोड़ता था
मिरे अंजाम की वो इब्तदा[2] थी

मुहब्बत मर गयी मुझको भी ग़म है
मिरे अच्छे दिनों की आशना[3] थी

जिसे छू लूँ मैं वो हो जाए सोना
तुझे देखा तो जाना बद्दुआ थी

मरीज़े-ख़्वाब[4] को तो अब शफ़ा[5] है
मगर दुनिया बड़ी कड़वी दवा थी

---

[1] हद; [2] शुरुआत; [3] परिचित; [4] सपने देखने का रोगी; [5] रोग से छुटकारा।

Ghazal

The extent of my desires was plain to see;
My goal turned out to be the road for me.

He left the herd and passed from glade to glade;
The price of his own musk the deer has paid.

I found my cherished dreams, but on the way
What things were lost to me I cannot say.

A child, I used to break my toys, but see!
This was the way the end began for me.

Love died, but how I grieved to see its end.
In better days it was my dearest friend.

Let all I touch now turn to gold! Untrue
The prayer I uttered when I looked at you.

Once sick from dreams, at last I found the cure;
But then life's draught was bitter to endure.

वो कमरा याद आता है

मैं जब भी
ज़िंदगी की चिलचिलाती धूप में तपकर
मैं जब भी
दूसरों के और अपने झूठ से थककर
मैं सबसे लड़ के खुद से हारके
जब भी उस इक कमरे में जाता था
वो हलके और गहरे कत्थई रंगों का इक कमरा
वो बेहद मेहरबाँ कमरा
जो अपनी नर्म मुट्ठी में मुझे ऐसे छुपा लेता था
जैसे कोई माँ
बच्चे को आँचल में छुपा ले
प्यार से डाँटे
ये क्या आदत है
जलती दोपहर में मारे मारे घूमते हो तुम
वो कमरा याद आता है
दबीज़[1] और ख़ासा भारी
कुछ ज़रा मुश्किल से खुलने वाला
वो शीशम का दरवाज़ा
कि जैसे कोई अक्खड़ बाप
अपने खुरदुरे सीने में
शफ़क़त[2] के समंदर को छुपाये हो

---

[1] ठोस; [2] स्नेह।

I Remember That Room

Whenever
I was scorched by the burning sun of life,
Whenever
I grew tired of my own lies and the lies of others,
Fighting with everyone, losing against myself,
I used to go into that room.
That one room with its light and dark brown colours,
That room, kind beyond all bounds,
Which used to tuck me up in its soft sleep
As a mother
Might hide a child in the folds of her dress,
Scolding with love:
'Now what a way to go on!
Wandering about in the midday sun!'
I remember that room,
That heavy, solid wooden door,
Hard to pull open
As if a stern father
In his rugged breast
Had hidden an ocean of tenderness.

वो कुर्सी
और उसके साथ वो जुड़वाँ बहन उसकी
वो दोनों
दोस्त थीं मेरी
वो इक गुस्ताख़ मुँहफट आईना
जो दिल का अच्छा था
वो बेहंगम[1] सी अलमारी
जो कोने में खड़ी
इक बूढ़ी अन्ना[2] की तरह
आईने को तन्बीह[3] करती थी
वो इक गुलदान[4]
नन्हा-सा
बहुत शैतान
उन दोनों पे हँसता था
दरीचा[5]
या ज़हानत[6] से भरी इक मुस्कुराहट
और दरीचे पर झुकी वो बेल
कोई सब्ज़[7] सरगोशी[8]
किताबें
ताक़ में और शेल्फ पर
संजीदा उस्तानी बनी बैठीं
मगर सब मुंतज़िर[9] इस बात की
मैं उनसे कुछ पूछूँ

---

[1] बेढंगी; [2] आया; [3] टोकना; [4] फूलदान; [5] खिड़की; [6] समझदारी; [7] हरे रंग की; [8] कानों में कही बात; [9] जो इंतज़ार करे।

40

That chair
With its twin sister,
Both of them
Were my friends.
That insolent, loud-mouthed mirror,
Which had a kind heart.
That clumsy wardrobe
Standing in the corner
Like an old nurse
Would reprove the mirror.
The flower vase
Quite tiny,
Very naughty;
Laughing at them both.
The window,
Or a knowing smile.
And the creeper, bending over the casement,
Some green whisper.
Books
In the alcoves or on the shelf
Sat like some serious school-ma'am;
But they waited for me
To ask them something.

सिरहाने
नींद का साथी
थकन का चारागर[1]
वो नर्म-दिल तकिया
मैं जिसकी गोद में सर रखके
छत को देखता था
छत की कड़ियों में
न जाने कितने अफ़सानों[2] की कड़ियाँ थीं
वो छोटी मेज़ पर
और सामने दीवार पर
आवेज़ाँ[3] तस्वीरें
मुझे अपनाईयत से और यक़ीं से देखतीं थीं
मुस्कुराती थीं
उन्हें शक भी नहीं था
एक दिन
मैं उनको ऐसे छोड़ जाऊँगा
मैं इक दिन यूँ भी जाऊँगा
कि फिर वापस न आऊँगा

मैं अब जिस घर में रहता हूँ
बहुत ही ख़ूबसूरत है
मगर अकसर यहाँ ख़ामोश बैठा याद करता हूँ
वो कमरा बात करता था।

---

[1] वैद-डॉक्टर; [2] कहानियों; [3] लगी हुई।

Pillows,
Companions of slumber;
Remedy for tiredness
That soft-hearted bolster
In whose lap I would rest my head
And gaze at the ceiling.
In the rafters of the roof
No one knows how many tales were begun.
Over the little table
On the facing wall
Hanging pictures
Used to look at me with affection and trust.
They smiled,
Never dreaming that
One day
I would leave like this;
One day I would depart,
Never to return.

The house where I live now
Is very, very fine.
But often I sit here in silence and remember
How that room would talk to me.

ऊँची इमारतों से मकां मेरा घिर गया
कुछ लोग मेरे हिस्से का सूरज भी खा गए

My house has been surrounded with high buildings;
I have been robbed of my share of the sun today.

ग़ज़ल

जंगल में घूमता है पहरों, फ़िक्रे-शिकार में दरिंदा
या अपने ज़ख़्म चाटता है, तनहा कछार में दरिंदा

बातों में दोस्ती का अमृत, सीनों में ज़हर नफ़रतों का
परबत पे फूल खिल रहे हैं, बैठा है ग़ार[1] में दरिंदा

ज़हनी यगानगत[2] के आगे, थीं ख़्वाहिशें ख़जिल[3] बदन की
चट्टान पर बैठा चाँद ताके, जैसे कुआँर में दरिंदा

गाँव से शहर आनेवाले, आए नदी पे जैसे प्यासे
था मुंतज़िर उन्हीं का कब से, इक रोज़गार में दरिंदा

मज़हब, न जंग, न सियासत, जाने न ज़ात-पात को भी
अपनी दरिंदगी के आगे, है किस शुमार[4] में दरिंदा

---

[1] गुफ़ा; [2] मानसिक रिश्ते; [3] लज्जित; [4] गिनती।

Ghazal

For hours in the jungle it stalks its prey—the wild beast
Or licks its wounds in a cavern alone—the wild beast.

In words the balm of friendship, in the breast the poison
of hate;
On the hill the flowers bloom; it sits in its cave—the wild
beast.

Before the unity of mind the desires of the body are
shamed;
On a rock it beholds the moon in its brightest month—
the wild beast.

From village to city they flocked like the thirsty to a
stream
So long it waited for them in the work they sought—the
wild beast.

Religion or war, caste or race, these things it does not
know
Before our savagery how do we judge the wild beast?

कौन-सा शे'र सुनाऊँ मैं तुम्हें, सोचता हूँ
नया मुब्हम[1] है बहुत और पुराना मुश्किल

---

[1] उलझा हुआ।

What verse shall I recite for you? I sometimes think
the new ones are obscure, the old ones far too hard.

भूख

आँख खुल गयी मेरी
हो गया मैं फिर ज़िन्दा
पेट के अँधेरों से
ज़हन[1] के धुँधलकों तक
एक साँप के जैसा
रेंगता ख़याल आया
आज तीसरा दिन है–आज तीसरा दिन है।

इक अजीब ख़ामोशी
मुंजमिद[2] है कमरे में
एक फ़र्श और इक छत
और चारदीवारें
मुझसे बेतआल्लुक़[3] सब
सब मिरे तमाशाई
सामने की खिड़की से
तेज़ धूप की किरनें
आ रही हैं बिस्तर पर
चुभ रही हैं चेहरे में
इस क़दर नुकीली हैं
जैसे रिश्तेदारों के
तंज़[4] मेरी गुरबत[5] पर

---

1 मस्तिष्क; 2 जमी हुई; 3 जिसका कोई वास्ता न हो; 4 व्यंग्य; 5 ग़रीबी।

50

Hunger

My eyes, they opened with the dawn
And once again I was alive.
From the darkness of the stomach
To the haze, which clouds the brain,
A thought came creeping
Like a snake:
Three days today! Three days today!

Silence gathers in the room,
Strangely frozen, not a sound;
Just one ceiling, just one floor,
Just four walls that crowd around.
All seems to be detached from me,
All spectators looking on.
Through the window opposite
The harsh rays of the morning sun
Flood and fall onto my bed,
Sting my face with pointed barbs,
Sharp as my relations' taunts
Hurled against my poverty.

आँख खुल गयी मेरी
आज खोखला हूँ मैं
सिर्फ़ ख़ोल बाक़ी है
आज मेरे बिस्तर में
लेटा है मेरा ढाँचा
अपनी मुर्दा आँखों से
देखता है कमरे को
आज तीसरा दिन है
आज तीसरा दिन है।

दोपहर की गर्मी में
बेइरादा क़दमों से
इक सड़क पे चलता हूँ
तंग-सी सड़क पर हैं
दोनों सम्त[1] दूकानें
ख़ाली ख़ाली आँखों से
हर दूकान का तख़्ता
सिर्फ़ देख सकता हूँ
अब पढ़ा नहीं जाता
लोग आते जाते हैं
पास से गुज़रते हैं
फिर भी कितने धुँधले हैं
सब हैं जैसे बेचेहरा
शोर इन दुकानों का

---

[1] ओर।

My eyes are open, but today
I am exhausted, Almost dead.
Of all I was a shell remains,
Lying empty
On my bed. My frame reposes
With dead eyes. I search and look
About my room.
Three days today!
Three days today!

In the midday heat I walk
With aimless steps
Along a street,
Along a narrow kind of street;
On both sides shops stand in a line.
The only things that I can see
Are boards displayed on every shop.
And now I cannot even read them.
People come, and people go,
Passing by me,
But how vague
As if they have no face at all.
The noisy shops

राह चलती इक गाली
रेडियो की आवाज़ें
दूर की सदाएँ हैं
आ रही हैं मीलों से
जो भी सुन रहा हूँ मैं
जो भी देखता हूँ मैं
ख़्वाब जैसा लगता है
है भी और नहीं भी है
दोपहर की गर्मी में
बेइरादा क़दमों से
इक सड़क पे चलता हूँ
सामने के नुक्कड़ पर
नल दिखायी देता है
सख़्त क्यों है ये पानी
क्यों गले में फँसता है
मेरे पेट में जैसे
घूँसा एक लगता है
आ रहा है चक्कर-सा
जिस्म पर पसीना है
अब सकत नहीं बाक़ी
आज तीसरा दिन है
आज तीसरा दिन है।

हर तरफ़ अँधेरा है
घाट पर अकेला हूँ
सीढ़ियाँ हैं पत्थर की

The rough, coarse words,
The jarring sound of radios,
Are echoes coming from afar,
Flooding in from miles around.
All I hear
And all I see
Greets me like some distant dream.
It is, and yet does not exist.
And in the midday heat I walk
With aimless steps
Along a street.
Then at the corner opposite
I see a pipe, I see a tap.
But why then is the water hard?
Why does it stick inside my throat?
It seems as if a blow is thrust
Against my stomach.
Now I feel that I might faint,
And sweat engulfs my body.
I have no strength left.
Three days today!
Three days today!

All around the darkness swells.
I am alone upon a quay.
Before me there are steps of stone

सीढ़ियों पे लेटा हूँ
अब मैं उठ नहीं सकता
आसमाँ को तकता हूँ
आसमाँ की थाली में
चाँद एक रोटी है
झुक रही हैं अब पलकें
डूबता है ये मंज़र[1]
है ज़मीन गर्दिश[2] में

मेरे घर में चूल्हा था
रोज़ खाना पकता था
रोटियाँ सुनहरी हैं
गर्म-गर्म ये खाना
खुल नहीं रहीं आँखें
क्या मैं मरने वाला हूँ
माँ अजीब थी मेरी
रोज़ अपने हाथों से
मुझको वो खिलाती थी
कौन सर्द[3] हाथों से
छू रहा है चेहरे को
इक निवाला[4] हाथी का
इक निवाला घोड़े का
इक निवाला भालू का
मौत है कि बेहोशी

---

[1] दृश्य; [2] चक्कर; [3] ठंडे; [4] कौर।

And I lie down upon the steps,
Unable now to raise myself.
I gaze up to the sky above
Served up upon the sky's vast dish,
The moon is shaped like a chapatti
And now my heavy eyelids droop,
The landscape sinks,
The earth revolves.

Once in my house there was a stove,
And food was cooked there every day.
Chapatties are like shining gold
And dinner's always piping hot.
My eyes are closing.
Will I die?
And what strange things my mother said,
As every day with her own hand
She used to feed me when she spoke.
Who puts his cold hands on my face?
'One mouthful for the elephant;
Another mouthful for the horse,
One more mouthful for the bear.'
Is this death?
Have I collapsed?

जो भी है ग़नीमत है
मौत है कि बेहोशी
जो भी है ग़नीमत है
आज तीसरा दिन था,
आज तीसरा दिन था।

Whatever, it is just as well.
Death or just unconsciousness.
Whatever, it is just as well.
Three days today!
Three days today!

खुशशक्ल[1] भी है वो, ये अलग बात है, मगर
हमको ज़हीन[2] लोग हमेशा अज़ीज़[3] थे

---

[1] अच्छी सूरतवाला; [2] समझदार; [3] प्यारे।

She even has a pretty face, but that's another thing.
Brains in people are the qualities I cherish most.

ग़ज़ल

हम तो बचपन में भी अकेले थे
सिर्फ़ दिल की गली में खेले थे

इक तरफ़ मोर्चे थे पलकों के
इक तरफ़ आँसुओं के रेले थे

थीं सजी हसरतें[1] दूकानों पर
ज़िंदगी के अजीब मेले थे

खुदकुशी क्या दुःखों का हल बनती
मौत के अपने सौ झमेले थे

ज़हनो-दिल आज भूखे मरते हैं
उन दिनों हमने फ़ाक़े झेले थे।

---

[1] इच्छाएँ।

Ghazal

In my childhood I was lonely every day;
The alley of my heart is where I used to play.

On one hand eyelashes would offer their defence,
But on the other gushing tears would find their way.

How wonderful and strange the fairgrounds of my life!
In all the shops desires in full were on display.

Could suicide provide the means of easing pain?
In death so many pitfalls and dilemmas lay.

In earlier days the pangs of fasting were endured.
The mind and heart, oppressed by hunger, die today.

हमको उठना तो मुँह अँधेरे था
लेकिन इक ख़्वाब हमको घेरे था

We should have risen at the crack of dawn,
But we slept on, engulfed in pleasant dreams.

बंजारा

मैं बंजारा
वक़्त के कितने शहरों से गुज़रा हूँ
लेकिन
वक़्त के इस इक शहर से जाते-जाते
मुड़के देख रहा हूँ
सोच रहा हूँ
तुमसे मेरा ये नाता भी टूट रहा है
तुमने मुझको छोड़ा था जिस शहर में आके
वक़्त का अब वो शहर भी मुझसे छूट रहा है

मुझको बिदा करने आए हैं
इस नगरी के सारे बासी
वो सारे दिन
जिनके कंधे पर सोती है
अब भी तुम्हारी ज़ुल्फ़ की खुशबू
सारे लम्हे
जिनके माथे पर हैं रौशन
अब भी तुम्हारे लम्स[1] का टीका
नम आँखों से
गुमसुम मुझको देख रहे हैं
मुझ को इन के दुख का पता है

[1] स्पर्श।

Banjara

I, a banjara,
Have passed through so many cities of time.
But
As I pass through this city of time,
I turn, I look and think
That even this bond we shared is breaking;
This city of time, in which you came
Then left me, is also ebbing far away from me.

All the people of the town have come
To bid farewell to me.
All those days
On whose shoulders sleeps
The perfume of your tresses even now;
All those moments
On whose forehead shines
The mark of your soft hand even now,
With tearful eyes
They look at me, numb and lost.
I understand their pain;

इन को मेरे ग़म की ख़बर है
लेकिन मुझ को हुक्मे सफ़र है
जाना होगा
वक़्त के अगले शहर मुझे अब जाना होगा

वक़्त के अगले शहर के सारे बाशिंदे[1]
सब दिन सब रातें
जो तुम से नावाक़िफ़[2] होंगे
वो कब मेरी बात सुनेंगे
मुझसे कहेंगे
जाओ अपनी राह लो राही
हमको कितने काम पड़े हैं
जो बीती सो बीत गयी
अब वो बातें क्यूँ दोहराते हो
कंधे पर ये झोली रक्खे
क्यूँ फिरते हो क्या पाते हो
मैं बेचारा
इक बंजारा
आवारा फिरते-फिरते जब थक जाऊँगा
तनहाई के टीले पर जाकर बैठूँगा
फिर जैसे पहचान के मुझको
इक बंजारा जान के मुझको
वक़्त के अगले शहर के
सारे नन्हे-मुन्ने भोले लम्हे

---

[1] निवासी; [2] अपरिचित।

They know the grief I feel,
But I am commanded to travel on.
I must depart,
And go on to the next city of time.

Those who dwell in the next city of time,
All those days and all those nights,
Who do not know you,
Will never listen to my words.
They will say to me:
'Go, traveller! Be on your way!
See how busy we are.
What has passed has passed.
Why do you repeat yourself?
With your bag on your shoulder
Why do you roam? What do you gain?'
I, a wretched fellow,
A banjara,
Wander aimlessly; and when I tire,
I shall go and sit on a mound of loneliness.
Then, as if they recognise me,
Knowing that I am a banjara,
From the next city of time,
All the tiny, simple moments

नंगे पाँव
दौड़े-दौड़े भागे-भागे आ जाएँगे
मुझको घेर के बैठेंगे
और मुझ से कहेंगे
क्यों बंजारे
तुम तो वक़्त के कितने शहरों से गुज़रे हो
उन शहरों की कोई कहानी हमें सुनाओ
उनसे कहूँगा
नन्हे लम्हो!
एक थी रानी . . .
सुन के कहानी
सारे नन्हे लम्हे
ग़मगीं[1] होकर मुझसे ये पूछेंगे
तुम क्यों उनके शहर न आयीं
लेकिन उनको बहला लूँगा
उनसे कहूँगा ये मत पूछो
आँखें मूँदो
और ये सोचो
तुम होतीं तो कैसा होता
तुम ये कहतीं
तुम वो कहतीं
तुम इस बात पे हैराँ होतीं
तुम उस बात पे कितनी हँसतीं
तुम होतीं तो ऐसा होता
तुम होतीं तो वैसा होता

---

[1] दुखी।

Will come,
Barefoot, hurrying and scurrying,
And sit around me,
And say:
'Tell us, banjara,
How many cities of time have you passed through?
Tell us the stories of those cities.'
And I shall say:
'Little moments!
Once upon a time
There was a queen . . .'
And after the story
All these little moments
Will be sad and ask me
Why you did not come to their city.
But I shall console them
And tell them: 'Do not ask.
Close your eyes
And think.'
If you were here, then what might be?
If you said this,
If you said that,
You would have been amazed by this.
How you would have laughed to hear that!
If you were here, then this might be.
If you were here, then that might be.

धीरे-धीरे
मेरे सारे नन्हे लम्हे
सो जाएँगे
और मैं
फिर हौले से उठकर
अपनी यादों की झोली कंधे पर रखकर
फिर चल दूँगा
वक़्त के अगले शहर की जानिब[1]
नन्हे लम्हों को समझाने
भोले लम्हों को बहलाने
यही कहानी फिर दोहराने
तुम होतीं तो ऐसा होता
तुम होतीं तो वैसा होता।

---

[1] तरफ़।

Softly, gently
All my little moments
Will fall asleep.
And I,
Slowly getting up once more,
Putting my bag of memories upon my shoulder,
Will take the road again
And head towards the next city of time
To explain to my tiny moments,
To console my innocent moments,
To tell my story once again.
If you were here, then this might be.
If you were here, then that might be.

ग़ज़ल

दिल में महक रहे हैं किसी आरज़ू के फूल
पलकों पे खिलनेवाले हैं शायद लहू के फूल

अब तक है कोई बात मुझे याद हर्फ़-हर्फ़[1]
अब तक मैं चुन रहा हूँ किसी गुफ़्तगू[2] के फूल

कलियाँ चटक रही थीं कि आवाज़ थी कोई
अब तक समाअतों[3] में हैं इक खुशगुलू[4] के फूल

मेरे लहू का रंग है हर नोके-ख़ार[5] पर
सहरा[6] में हर तरफ़ हैं मिरी जुस्तजू[7] के फूल

दीवाने कल जो लोग थे फूलों के इश्क़ में
अब उनके दामनों में भरे हैं रफ़ू[8] के फूल

---

[1] एक-एक अक्षर; [2] बात-चीत; [3] सुनने की शक्ति; [4] अच्छी आवाज़ वाला;
[5] कांटे की नोक; [6] वीराना; [7] तलाश; [8] पैबंद।

Ghazal

The heart is perfumed by desire and all its flowers;
Perhaps the lashes will be decked by blood's own flowers.

Yes, I remember all we said then word for word;
Of some dear conversation I still pluck the flowers.

Was it the sound of bursting buds? Was it a voice?
I still hear someone talking sweetly like the flowers.

The tip of every thorn is reddened with my blood;
The traces of my searching are the desert flowers.

In love with flowers some lost their reason yesterday;
Today their ragged collars have been stitched by flowers.

सब का ख़ुशी से फ़ासला एक क़दम है
हर घर में बस एक ही कमरा कम है

All of us are just one step from happiness;
In every house we always seem to lack one room.

ग़ज़ल

सूखी टहनी तनहा चिड़िया फीका चाँद
आँखों के सहरा[1] में एक नमी का चाँद

उस माथे को चूमे कितने दिन बीते
जिस माथे की ख़ातिर था इक टीका चाँद

पहले तू लगती थी कितनी बेगाना
कितना मुब्हम[2] होता है पहली का चाँद

कम हो कैसे इन खुशियों से तेरा ग़म
लहरों में कब बहता है नदी का चाँद

आओ अब हम इसके भी टुकड़े कर लें
ढाका, रावलपिंडी और दिल्ली का चाँद

---

[1] वीराना; [2] धुँधला।

Ghazal

A withered branch, a lonely bird, a pale moon,
And in the desert of the eyes a watery moon.

How long it is, how many days since I last kissed
That forehead, upon which the caste-mark was the moon.

At first you seemed detached, so hard to find.
How difficult it is to see the month's first moon.

If I feel joy, how can my grief for you grow less?
It never flowed upon the wave, the river's moon.

Now come with me and let us share this out as well
Dhaka, Rawalpindi, Delhi—their bright moon!

अपनी वजहे-बरबादी सुनिये तो मज़े की है
ज़िंदगी से यूँ खेले जैसे दूसरे की है

It might provide you some amusement
To hear the reason for my fall.
I've played with life, as if my life
Does not belong to me at all.

एक मोहरे का सफ़र

जब वो कम उम्र ही था
उसने ये जान लिया था कि अगर जीना है
बड़ी चालाकी से जीना होगा
आँख की आख़िरी हद तक है बिसाते-हस्ती[1]
और वो मामूली सा इक मोहरा है
एक इक ख़ाना बहुत सोच के चलना होगा
बाज़ी आसान नहीं थी उसकी
दूर तक चारों तरफ़ फैले थे
मोहरे
जल्लाद
निहायत सफ़्फ़ाक[2]
सख़्त बेरहम
बहुत ही चालाक
अपने क़ब्ज़े में लिए
पूरी बिसात[3]
उसके हिस्से में फ़क़त[4] मात लिए
वो जिधर जाता
उसे मिलता था
हर नया ख़ाना नई घात लिए
वो मगर बचता रहा
चलता रहा

---

[1] जीवन के शतरंज की बिसात; [2] बेदर्द; [3] शतरंज; [4] केवल।

The Journey of a Pawn

When he was still quite young
He learnt that if you want to stay alive
You have to be as cunning as you can.
The board extends as far as the eye can see,
And he is just an ordinary pawn.
He has to go from square to square, with utmost thought.
The game he played was never easy;
Far and wide, in all directions were deployed
Pawns
Heartless,
Bloodthirsty in the extreme,
Hard, merciless,
And very cunning,
Taking in their control
The entire board;
Intent only upon checkmating him.
Wherever he moved
He encountered
Each new square concealing a new ambush.
But he survived,
He progressed,

एक घर
दूसरा घर
तीसरा घर
पास आया कभी औरों के
कभी दूर हुआ
वो मगर बचता रहा
चलता रहा
गो[1] कि मामूली सा मोहरा था मगर जीत गया
यूँ वो इक रोज़ बड़ा मोहरा बना
अब वो महफ़ूज़[2] है इक ख़ाने में
इतना महफ़ूज़ कि दुश्मन तो अलग
दोस्त भी पास नहीं आ सकते

उसके इक हाथ में है जीत उसकी
दूसरे हाथ में तनहाई है।

---

[1] यद्यपि; [2] सुरक्षित।

One house,
Another house,
A third house.
Sometimes he drew near to others,
Sometimes he moved far away.
But he survived,
He progressed.
Although he was a humble pawn, he won.
And so, one day, he became a great pawn,
Now he is safe within one square;
So safe that let alone his enemies
Not even his friends can approach him.

In one hand he clasps victory.
In the other he clutches loneliness.

मदर टेरेसा

ए माँ टेरेसा
मुझको तेरी अज़मत[1] से इनकार नहीं है
जाने कितने
सूखे लब और वीराँ आँखें
जाने कितने
थके बदन और ज़ख़्मी रूहें
कूड़ाघर में रोटी का इक टुकड़ा ढूँढते नंगे बच्चे
फुटपाथों पर गलते सड़ते बुड्ढे कोढ़ी
जाने कितने
बेघर बेदर[2] बेकस[3] इनसाँ
जाने कितने
टूटे कुचले बेबस इनसाँ
तेरी छाँवों में
जीने की हिम्मत पाते हैं
इनको अपने होने की जो सज़ा मिली है
उस होने की सज़ा से
थोड़ी सी ही सही
मोहलत[4] पाते हैं
तेरा लम्स[5] मसीहा है
और तेरा करम है एक समंदर
जिसका कोई पार नहीं है
ए माँ टेरेसा

---

[1] महानता; [2] बिना ठिकाना; [3] असहाय; [4] फुरसत; [5] स्पर्श।

Mother Teresa

Mother Teresa!
I cannot deny your greatness.
Who can tell how many
Dry lips and vacant eyes,
Who knows how many
Exhausted bodies and wounded spirits,
Naked children searching for a crust on rubbish tips,
Old lepers, putrefying and rotting on the pavement;
Who knows how many
Destitute human beings, homeless, without roots,
Broken, trampled, helpless human beings
In your shadow
Find the strength to live?
The punishment they have received just for being,
From that punishment for their existence
They find some respite,
However small.
The touch of your hand is their Messiah,
And your kindness is an ocean,
Which knows no bounds.
Mother Teresa!

मुझको तेरी अज़मत से इनकार नहीं है
मैं ठहरा खुदग़र्ज़
बस इक अपनी ही ख़ातिर जीनेवाला
मैं तुझसे किस मुँह से पूछूँ
तूने कभी ये क्यूँ नही पूछा
किसने इन बदहालों को बदहाल किया है
तूने कभी ये क्यूँ नहीं सोचा
कौन-सी ताक़त
इनसानों से जीने का हक़ छीनके
उनको फुटपाथों और कूड़ाघरों तक पहुँचाती है
तूने कभी ये क्यूँ नहीं देखा
वही निज़ामे-ज़र[1]
जिसने इन भूखों से रोटी छीनी है
तिरे कहने पर
भूखों के आगे
कुछ टुकड़े डाल रहा है
तूने कभी ये क्यूँ नहीं चाहा
नंगे बच्चे
बुड्ढे कोढ़ी
बेबस इनसाँ
इस दुनिया से
अपने जीने का हक़ माँगें
जीने की ख़ैरात न माँगें
ऐसा क्यूँ है
इक जानिब[2] मज़लूम[3] से तुझको हमदर्दी है

---

[1] अर्थव्यवस्था; [2] तरफ; [3] जुल्म सहनेवाला।

I cannot deny your greatness.
But I am selfish;
All I do is live for myself.
So who am I to ask you this?
Why have you never asked
Who has made these miserable people so wretched?
Why have you never thought
What power
Has robbed humans of their right to live,
Bringing them onto the pavements and the rubbish tips?
Why have you never seen
That this very system of gold and riches,
Which snatches the bread from the hungry
Because of your word,
Throws down scraps
Before the starving?
Why have you never wished
That naked children,
Old lepers,
Helpess humans
Should ask from this world,
Their right to live
And not just charity to live upon?
Why is it that
On one hand you sympathise with the oppressed

दूसरी जानिब
ज़ालिम से भी आर[1] नहीं है
लेकिन सच है
ऐसी बातें
मैं तुझसे किस मुँह से पूछूँ
पूछूँगा तो
मुझ पर भी वो ज़िम्मेदारी आ जाएगी
जिससे मैं बचता आया हूँ

बेहतर है ख़ामोश रहूँ मैं
और अगर कुछ कहना हो तो
यही कहूँ मैं
ए माँ टेरेसा
मुझको तेरी अज़मत से इनकार नहीं है।

---

[1] संकोच।

But on the other
You are not abashed by their oppressor?
But this is true,
How dare
I ask you such things?
If I ask,
Then I shall also have that responsibility
From which so far I have escaped.

Perhaps it is better to keep silent,
And if there is anything to say,
Let me say this one thing:
Mother Teresa!
I cannot deny your greatness.

इस शहर में जीने के अंदाज़ निराले हैं
होठों पे लतीफ़े हैं आवाज़ में छाले हैं

The ways of the city are fine. Rejoice!
Jokes on the lips and blisters in the voice.

फ़साद से पहले

आज इस शहर में
हर शख़्स हिरासाँ[1] क्यूँ है
चेहरे.
क्यों फ़क़[2] हैं
गली कूचों में
किसलिए चलती है
ख़ामोशो-सरासीमा[3] हवा
आश्ना[4] आँखों पे भी
अजनबियत की ये बारीक सी झिल्ली क्यूँ है
शहर
सन्नाटे की ज़ंजीरों में
जकड़ा हुआ मुलज़िम[5] सा नज़र आता है
इक्का-दुक्का
कोई रहगीर गुज़र जाता है
ख़ौफ़ की गर्द से
क्यूँ धुँधला है सारा मंज़र
शाम की रोटी कमाने के लिए
घर से निकले तो हैं कुछ लोग
मगर
मुड़ के क्यूँ देखते हैं घर की तरफ़
आज

---

[1] डरा हुआ; [2] उतरे हुए; [3] चुप और घबराई; [4] परिचित; [5] अपराधी।

Before the Riot

Today in this city
Why is everyone afraid?
Why
Are faces pale?
In the alleys and lanes
Why is there
Silence in the stupefied air?
And over familiar eyes
Why is there a veil of strangeness?
The city
Is hushed in its chains,
Looking like a fettered criminal.
Here and there
Someone passes by.
Why is the scene clouded
By the dust of fear?
To earn their evening meal
A few people emerge from their houses;
But why do they turn and look back to their home?
Today

बाज़ार में भी
जाना पहचाना सा वो शोर नहीं
सब यूँ चलते हैं कि जैसे
ये ज़मीं काँच की है
हर नज़र
नज़रों से कतराती है
बात
खुलकर नहीं हो पाती है
साँस रोके हुए
हर चीज़ नज़र आती है
आज
ये शहर इक सहमे हुए बच्चे की तरह
अपनी परछाई से भी डरता है

जंत्री देखो
मुझे लगता है
आज त्यौहार कोई है शायद।

Even in the bazaar
The familiar noise is absent.
Everyone walks as if
The ground were made of glass.
Every glance
Avoids the eyes of others.
Nothing
Can be expressed openly.
Everything seems
To hold its breath.
Today
The city is like a frightened child,
Afraid even of its own shadow.

Look at the calendar.
I think
Perhaps there is some festival today.

ग़ज़ल

वो ढल रहा है तो ये भी रंगत बदल रही है
ज़मीन सूरज की उँगलियों से फिसल रही है

जो मुझको ज़िंदा जला रहे हैं वो बेख़बर हैं
कि मेरी ज़ंजीर धीरे-धीरे पिघल रही है

मैं क़त्ल तो हो गया तुम्हारी गली में लेकिन
मिरे लहु से तुम्हारी दीवार गल रही है

न जलने पाते थे जिसके चूल्हे भी हर सवेरे
सुना है कल रात से वो बस्ती भी जल रही है

मैं जानता हूँ कि ख़ामशी[1] में ही मस्लहत[2] है
मगर यही मस्लहत मिरे दिल को खल रही है

कभी तो इंसान ज़िंदगी की करेगा इज़्ज़त
ये एक उम्मीद आज भी दिल में पल रही है

---

[1] ख़ामोशी; [2] समझदारी।

98

Ghazal

Evening falls, the colours change and run,
The earth slips through the fingers of the sun.

They're burning me alive but do not know
My chains are slowly melting in the glow.

And I was slaughtered in your street one day,
But with my blood your walls will wash away.

They could not even set their stoves alight;
I've heard their town's been burning since last night.

All virtue comes from silence, so I'm told,
But that great virtue makes my blood run cold.

One day, life will be honoured by mankind.
This one desire I nurture in my mind.

फ़साद के बाद

गहरा सन्नाटा है
कुछ मकानों से ख़ामोश उठता हुआ
गाढ़ा काला धुआँ
मैल दिल में लिए
हर तरफ़ दूर तक फैलता जाता है
गहरा सन्नाटा है

लाश की तरह बेजान है रास्ता
एक टूटा हुआ ठेला
उलटा पड़ा
अपने पहिये हवा में उठाए हुए
आसमानों को हैरत से तकता है
जैसे कि जो भी हुआ
उसका अब तक यक़ीं इसको आया नहीं
गहरा सन्नाटा है

एक उजड़ी दूकाँ
चीख के बाद मुँह
जो खुला का खुला रह गया
अपने टूटे किवाड़ों से वो
दूर तक फैले
चूड़ी के टुकड़ों को

After the Riot

There is a deathly hush.
From some houses rises silent,
Thick black smoke,
Its heart sullied,
Spreading far and wide, engulfing everything.
There is a deathly hush.

The street—lifeless as a corpse.
A broken barrow
Turned upside down,
Its wheels in the air,
Gazes at the heavens in amazement,
As if it still cannot believe
What happened.
There is a deathly hush.

A smashed up shop,
Like a mouth wide open
After a scream,
Looks from its broken doors
At the fragments of bangles
Scattered afar

हसरतज़दा[1] नज़रों से देखती है
कि कल तक यही शीशे
इस पोपले के मुँह में
सौ रंग के दाँत थे
गहरा सन्नाटा है

गहरे सन्नाटे ने अपने मंज़र से यूँ बात की
सुन ले उजड़ी दुकाँ
ए सुलगते मकाँ
टूटे ठेले
तुम्हीं बस नहीं हो अकेले
यहाँ और भी हैं
जो ग़ारत[2] हुए हैं
हम इनका भी मातम करेंगे
मगर पहले उनको तो रो लें
कि जो लूटने आए थे
और ख़ुद लुट गए
क्या लुटा
इसकी उनको ख़बर ही नहीं
कमनज़र हैं
कि सदियों की तहज़ीब पर
उन बेचारों की कोई नज़र ही नहीं।

---

[1] उदास आशा से भरी नज़र; [2] बरबाद।

With longing eyes, thinking
That yesterday these pieces of glass
Were teeth of a myriad colours
In this toothless mouth.
There is a deathly hush.

The silence speaks to the scene around:
'Listen, smashed up shop,
Smouldering house,
Broken barrow!
You are not the only ones;
There are others as well,
Who have been destroyed.
For them also we shall mourn,
But first let us weep for those,
Who came here to loot
And were themselves robbed.
They have no idea
Of what they have lost.
They see little,
For on this age-old civilisation
Those miserable people
Have no view at all.'

ग़ज़ल

ख़्वाब के गाँव में पले हैं हम
पानी छलनी में ले चले हैं हम

छाछ फूँकें कि अपने बचपन में
दूध से किस तरह जले हैं हम

खुद हैं अपने सफ़र की दुश्वारी[1]
अपने पैरों के आबले[2] हैं हम

तू तो मत कह हमें बुरा दुनियाँ
तूने ढाला है और ढले हैं हम

क्यूँ हैं कब तक हैं किसकी ख़ातिर हैं
बड़े संजीदा[3] मसअले[4] हैं हम

---

[1] मुश्किल; [2] छाले; [3] गंभीर; [4] समस्या।

Ghazal

In a village of dreams we used to live,
Fetching   water   in   a   sieve.

Blow on the froth; that's how we learnt
In childhood lips by milk get burnt.

It's we who stop and block the street.
We are the blisters on our feet.

Dear world! Be kind. We're not to blame.
You fashioned us, and hence we came.

Why are we here? For whom? How far?
Complicated—that's what we are!

गली में शोर था मातम था और होता क्या
मैं घर में था मगर इस गुल[1] में कोई सोता क्या

---

[1] शोर।

In the alley shouts and moans and cries.
I was at home, but who could close his eyes?

ग़ज़ल

ग़म होते हैं जहाँ ज़हानत होती है
दुनिया में हर शय[1] की क़ीमत होती है

अकसर वो कहते हैं वो बस मेरे हैं
अकसर क्यूँ कहते हैं हैरत होती है

तब हम दोनों वक़्त चुरा कर लाते थे
अब मिलते हैं जब भी फुरसत होती है

अपनी महबूबा में अपनी माँ देखें
बिन माँ के लड़कों की फ़ितरत[2] होती है

इक कश्ती में एक क़दम ही रखते हैं
कुछ लोगों की ऐसी आदत होती है

---

[1] चीज़; [2] प्रकृति।

Ghazal

Where intellect exists there's always strife,
But all things have conditions in this life.

She often says that she belongs to me.
But why so often? That I cannot see.

We used to steal what time we had for pleasure,
But now we meet when we can find the leisure.

They see their mother in their sweetheart's frame.
Without a mother boys all act the same.

One step into a boat, that's all they place.
They act like that, some people of our race.

आज की दुनिया में जीने का क़रीना[1] समझो
जो मिलें प्यार से उन लोगों को ज़ीना[2] समझो

---

[1] तरीका; [2] सीढ़ी।

The way to live in this wide world is very clear:
Count those who greet you with their love a useful stair!

ग़ज़ल

हमसे दिलचस्प कभी सच्चे नहीं होते हैं
अच्छे लगते हैं मगर अच्छे नहीं होते हैं

चाँद में बुढ़िया बुजुर्गों में ख़ुदा को देखें
भोले अब इतने तो ये बच्चे नहीं होते हैं

कोई याद आये हमें कोई हमें याद करे
और सब होता है ये क़िस्से नहीं होते हैं

कोई मंज़िल हो बहुत दूर ही होती है मगर
रास्ते वापसी के लंबे नहीं होते हैं

आज तारीख़[1] तो दोहराती है ख़ुद को लेकिन
इसमें बेहतर जो थे वो हिस्से नहीं होते हैं।

---

[1] इतिहास।

Ghazal

Interesting but never truthful, you and me!
We seem quite good, but we're not good at all, you see!

A man lives on the moon, and God in wise old men!
No! The young aren't quite so gullible as they were then.

Remembering someone, someone else remembering me.
I may have everything but only this can't be.

It may take endless time to reach a distant goal,
But slipping back does not take any time at all.

They say that history repeats itself today,
But then the best parts always seem to go astray.

कम से कम उसको देख लेते थे
अब के सैलाब में वो पुल भी गया

At least I could look at her, but now
The flood has washed even that bridge away.

मुअम्मा[1]

हम दोनों जो हर्फ़[2] थे
हम इक रोज़ मिले
इक लफ़्ज़[3] बना
और हमने इक माने[4] पाए
फिर जाने क्या हम पर गुज़री
और अब यूँ है
तुम इक हर्फ़ हो
इक ख़ाने में
मैं इक हर्फ़ हूँ
इक ख़ाने में
बीच में
कितने लम्हों के ख़ाने ख़ाली हैं
फिर से कोई लफ़्ज़ बने
और हम दोनों इक माने पाएँ
ऐसा हो सकता है
लेकिन
सोचना होगा
इन ख़ाली ख़ानों में हमको भरना क्या है।

---

[1] पहेली; [2] अक्षर; [3] शब्द; [4] अर्थ।

Riddle

The two of us were once just letters.
We met one day
And a word was made.
We found a meaning,
Then something happened.
And now
You are a letter
In one square;
I am a letter
In one square.
In between
How many squares of moments lie empty!
Let us make another word.
And let us find another meaning.
It could be so,
But we have to think
How we can fill those empty squares.

ऐ सफ़र इतना रायगाँ[1] तो न जा
न हो मंज़िल कहीं तो पहुँचा दे

---

[1] बेकार ।

My journey! Be not wasted, do not be in vain. Just lead me somewhere, even if not to the end.

उलझन

करोड़ों चेहरे
और उनके पीछे
करोड़ों चेहरे
ये रास्ते हैं कि भिड़ के छत्ते
ज़मीन जिस्मों से ढक गई है
क़दम तो क्या तिल भी धरने की अब जगह नहीं है
ये देखता हूँ तो सोचता हूँ
कि अब जहाँ हूँ
वहीं सिमट के खड़ा रहूँ मैं
मगर करूँ क्या
कि जानता हूँ
कि रुक गया तो
जो भीड़ पीछे से आ रही है
वो मुझको पैरों तले कुचल देगी, पीस देगी
तो अब जो चलता हूँ मैं
तो खुद मेरे अपने पैरों में आ रहा है
किसी का सीना
किसी का बाजू
किसी का चेहरा
चलूँ
तो औरों पे ज़ुल्म ढाऊँ
रुकूँ
तो औरों के ज़ुल्म झेलूँ

Perplexity

Millions of faces
And following them
Millions of faces.
Are these streets or hornets' nests.
The earth is covered with bodies.
No place to walk, no room to squeeze by.
I look at this and think
That I might as well remain
Rooted where I am.
But what can I do?
Because I know
That if I stop,
The crowd behind me
Will trample me under its feet and crush me.
So now, as I walk,
Under my own feet is
Someone's chest,
Someone's arm,
Someone's face.
If I walk on,
I shall oppress others.
If I stop,
I shall suffer oppression.

ज़मीर[1]
तुझको तो नाज़ है अपनी मुंसिफ़ी[2] पर
ज़रा सुनूँ तो
कि आज क्या तेरा फ़ैसला है।

---

[1] अंतरात्मा; [2] न्यायप्रियता।

My conscience!

You are so proud of your sense of justice,

So tell me:

What decision have you reached today?

जहन्नुमी[1]

मैं अकसर सोचता हूँ
ज़हन[2] की तारीक[3] गलियों में
दहकता और पिघलता
धीरे-धीरे आगे बढ़ता
ग़म का ये लावा
अगर चाहूँ
तो रुक सकता है
मेरे दिल की कच्ची खाल पर रक्खा ये अंगारा
अगर चाहूँ
तो बुझ सकता है
लेकिन
फिर ख़याल आता है
मेरे सारे रिश्तों में पड़ी
सारी दरारों से
गुज़र के आनेवाली बर्फ़ से ठंडी हवा
और मेरी हर पहचान पर सर्दी का ये मौसम
कहीं ऐसा न हो
इस जिस्म को, इस रूह को ही मुंजमिद[4] कर दे

मैं अकसर सोचता हूँ
ज़हन की तारीक गलियों में

---

1 नारकीय; 2 मस्तिष्क; 3 अँधेरी; 4 स्थिर।

Infernal

I often think
That the lava of grief,
Flaming and melting,
Slowly creeping forward
In the dark lanes of my mind,
If I wished,
Could be stemmed;
The embers lying on the raw skin of my heart,
If I wished,
Might be extinguished.
But
Then I think
That the wind, blowing colder than ice
Through the chinks
Of all my relationships,
The chill weather settling on all my friendships
Might, heaven forbid!
Freeze this body and this soul.

I often think
That the lava of grief

दहकता और पिघलता
धीरे-धीरे आगे बढ़ता
ग़म का ये लावा
अज़ीयत[1] है
मगर फिर भी ग़नीमत[2] है
इसी से रूह में गर्मी
बदन में ये हरारत[3] है
ये ग़म मेरी ज़रूरत है
मैं अपने ग़म से ज़िंदा हूँ

---

[1] तकलीफ़; [2] ठीक; [3] गर्मी।

Flaming and melting
Slowly creeping forward
In the dark lanes of my mind,
Is torment.
But at least it is something
From which warmth reaches my soul,
From which heat enters my body.
This grief is my necessity.
Because of my grief I am alive.

बीमार की रात

दर्द बेरहम है
जल्लाद है दर्द
दर्द कुछ कहता नहीं
सुनता नहीं
दर्द बस होता है
दर्द का मारा हुआ
रौंदा हुआ
जिस्म तो अब हार गया
रूह ज़िद्दी है
लड़े जाती है
हाँफती
काँपती
घबराई हुई
दर्द के ज़ोर से
थर्राई हुई
जिस्म से लिपटी है
कहती है
नहीं छोड़ूँगी
मौत
चौखट पे खड़ी है कब से
सब्र से देख रही है उसको
आज की रात
न जाने क्या हो

128

A Night of Illness

The pain is merciless.
How cruel the pain!
The pain says nothing,
Hears nothing.
Just pain.
Defeated by pain,
Crushed,
The body has lost its battle.
The spirit is stubborn;
It goes on fighting,
Heaves,
Trembles,
Panics.
At the onslaught of pain
It shakes;
Enfolding the body
It says:
'I shall not give in!'
How long has death
Been standing by the lintel,
Eyeing it patiently?
This night
Who knows what will happen?

ग़ज़ल

ये तसल्ली है कि हैं नाशाद[1] सब
मैं अकेला ही नहीं बरबाद सब

सबकी ख़ातिर हैं यहाँ सब अजनबी
और कहने को हैं घर आबाद सब

भूलके सब रंजिशें[2] सब एक हैं
मैं बताऊँ सबको होगा याद सब

सबको दावाऐ-वफ़ा सबको यक़ीं
इस अदाकारी में हैं उस्ताद सब

शहर के हाकिम का ये फ़रमान है
क़ैद में कहलायेंगे आज़ाद सब

चार लफ़्ज़ों में कहो जो भी कहो
उसको कब फुरसत सुने फ़रियाद सब

तल्खियाँ[3] कैसे न हों अशआर[4] में
हम पे जो गुज़री हमें है याद सब

---

[1] नाख़ुश; [2] दुश्मनी; [3] कड़वाहटें; [4] शेर का बहुवचन।

130

Ghazal

It's comforting that everyone is sad;
I'm not the only one whose life is bad.

Strangers to each other everyone;
Communities exist in name alone.

Forgetting grudges we can all unite;
I'll tell you this: we all recall our spite.

Honesty we claim; we say we know.
And everyone's a master of this show.

The rulers of this town make this decree:
'Let everyone in prison be called free.'

Say what you have to say with great restraint;
She won't have time to hear a long complaint.

Bitter verses, full of misery.
But I remember what became of me.

ग़ज़ल

मैं पा सका न कभी इस ख़लिश[1] से छुटकारा
वो मुझसे जीत भी सकता था जाने क्यों हारा

बरस के खुल गए आँसू निथर गई है फ़िज़ा
चमक रहा है सरे-शाम[2] दर्द का तारा

किसी की आँख से टपका था इक अमानत है
मिरी हथेली पे रक्खा हुआ ये अंगारा

जो पर समेटे तो इक शाख़ भी नहीं पाई
खुले थे पर तो मिरा आसमान था सारा

वो साँप छोड़ दे इसना ये मैं भी कहता हूँ
मगर न छोड़ेंगे लोग उसको गर न फुंकारा।

---

[1] उलझन; [2] शाम होते ही।

Ghazal

I could never find relief; the smarting grows.
He could have won from me, but why he lost, who knows!

The sky grew clearer and tears stooped like the rain,
And on the evening sky arose the star of pain.

It dripped from someone's eye, and now here is the test:
Upon my outstretched palm its glowing embers rest.

My wings were clipped; for me the branch was far too high.
But when wings were spread to me belonged the sky.

Now let the snake give up its biting—I agree.
But if it did not hiss, would people let it free.

लो देख लो ये इश्क़ है ये वस्ल[1] है ये हिज्र[2]
अब लौट चलें आओ बहुत काम पड़ा है

---

[1] मिलन; [2] जुदाई।

See! Here is love and union and separation!
So let's go back; there's much work to be done.

ग़ज़ल

मैं ख़ुद भी सोचता हूँ ये क्या मेरा हाल है
जिसका जवाब चाहिए वो क्या सवाल है

घर से चला तो दिल के सिवा पास कुछ न था
क्या मुझसे खो गया है मुझे क्या मलाल[1] है

आसूदगी[2] से दिल के सभी दाग़ धुल गये
लेकिन वो कैसे जाए जो शीशे में बाल है

बेदस्तोपा[3] हूँ आज तो इल्ज़ाम किसको दूँ
कल मैंने ही बुना था ये मेरा ही जाल है

फिर कोई ख़्वाब देखूँ, कोई आरज़ू करूँ
अब ऐ दिले-तबाह[4] तिरा क्या ख़याल है

---

[1] दुख; [2] खुशहाली; [3] मजबूर; [4] बरबाद दिल।

Ghazal

I also wonder how I feel and what I do.
What is the question that I need an answer to?

I left my home and only had my heart with me;
So what have I lost, and why am I in misery?

Contentment cleansed my heart and washed away its stains,
But even now upon the glass a crack remains.

If I am helpless, whom shall I accuse today?
The web in which I'm caught—I wove it yesterday.

Another dream? A fresh desire? Where shall I start?
Just tell me any thoughts you have, my broken heart!

वह शक्ल पिघली तो हर शय में ढल गई जैसे
अजीब बात हुई है उसे भुलाने में

The image melted and ran into everything.
How strange it seemed to me forgetting her.

शिकस्त[1]

स्याह[2] टीले पे तनहा खड़ा वो सुनता है
फ़िज़ा में गूँजती अपनी शिकस्त की आवाज़
निगह[3] के सामने
मैदाने-कारज़ार[4] जहाँ
जियाले[5] ख़्वाबों के पामाल[6] और ज़ख़्मी बदन
पड़े हैं बिखरे हुए चारों सम्त[7]
बेतरतीब[8]
बहुत से मर चुके
और जिनकी साँस चलती है
सिसक रहे हैं
किसी लम्हा मरनेवाले हैं
ये उसके ख़्वाब
ये उसकी सिपाह[9]
उसके जरी[10]
चले थे घर से तो कितनी ज़मीन जीती थी
झुकाए कितने थे मग़रूर[11] बादशाहों के सर
फ़सीलें[12] टूट के गिरके सलाम करती थीं
पहुँचना शर्त थी
थर्रा के आप खुलते थे
तमाम क़िलओं के दरवाज़े

---

[1] हार; [2] काला; [3] नज़र; [4] रणभूमि; [5] निडर; [6] रौंदे हुए; [7] तरफ़; [8] अस्त-व्यस्त; [9] फ़ौज; [10] बहादुर; [11] अभिमानी; [12] किले की दीवारें।

Defeat

He stands alone upon a high black mound and hears
The echoes in the air, the voice of his defeat.
Before his eyes
The battlefield spread out.
His valiant dreams are crushed and wounded bodies lie
Scattered, tossed around the field
On every side.
So many dead!
And those, who still have some breath left
Are sobbing,
Waiting for the hand of death to strike.
These are his dreams,
This is his army,
Stalwart men;
They left their homes, and on their way took many lands,
So many overweening royal heads they bowed,
And ramparts crumbled, fell, submitting at their feet.
All they had to do was arrive
And quaking, shuddering gates
Were opened
Of every fort,

सारे महलों के दर

नज़र में उन दिनों मंज़र बहुत सजीला था
ज़मीं सुनहरी थी
और आसमान नीला था
मगर थी ख़्वाबों के लश्कर में किसको इसकी ख़बर
हर एक किस्से का इक इख़तिताम[1] होता है
हज़ार लिख दे कोई फ़तह[2] ज़र्रें ज़र्रें पर
मगर शिकस्त का भी इक मुक़ाम होता है
उफ़क़[3] पे चींटियाँ रेंगीं
ग़नीम[4] फ़ौजों ने
वो देखता है
कि ताज़ा कुमक बुलाई है
शिकारी निकले हैं उसके शिकार की ख़ातिर
ज़मीन कहती है
ये नरग़ा[5] तंग होने को है
हवाएँ कहती हैं
अब वापसी का मौसम है
प[6] वापसी का कहाँ रास्ता बनाया था
जब आ रहा था कहाँ ये ख़्याल आया था
पलट के देखता है
सामने समंदर है
किनारे कुछ भी नहीं
सिर्फ़ एक राख का ढेर
ये उसकी कश्ती है

---

[1] अंत; [2] विजय; [3] क्षितिज; [4] दुश्मन; [5] घेरा; [6] पर।

Of every palace
In those days every sight brought pleasure to their eyes.
The earth was bathed in gold,
The sky was clothed in blue.
But in this regiment of dreams who could have known
That every story, every fable has its end?
Let victory be heralded a thousand times,
But there will always be a moment of defeat.
Far off like swarming ants
The enemy amassed.
He sees
They summon reinforcements to their side.
These hunters have come out to stalk their awesome prey.
The earth cries out:
'The siege is near and closing in!'
The winds call:
'Now the time has come to sound retreat.'
But there was never any plan of turning back.
As he advanced, he never gave a thought to this.
He looks around.
Before him is the open sea,
And nothing on the shore
Except a heap of dust.
That was his ship,

कल उसने खुद जलाई थी

क़रीब आने लगीं क़ातिलों की आवाज़ें
स्याह टीले पे तनहा खड़ा वो सुनता है।

Which yesterday he put to flame.

The shouts of murderers draw nearer, ever close.
He stands alone upon a high black mound and hears . . .

वो नहर एक क़िस्सा है दुनिया के वास्ते
फ़रहाद ने तराशा था ख़ुद को चटान पर

The stream is just one story for the world
Farhad engraved his name upon the rock.

ग़ज़ल

सच ये है बेकार हमें ग़म होता है
जो चाहा था दुनिया में कम होता है

ढलता सूरज फैला जंगल रस्ता गुम
हमसे पूछो कैसा आलम होता है

ग़ैरों को कब फ़ुरसत है दुख देने की
जब होता है कोई हमदम होता है

ज़ख़्म तो हमने इन आँखों से देखे हैं
लोगों से सुनते हैं मरहम होता है

ज़हन की शाख़ों पर अशआर[1] आ जाते हैं
जब तेरी यादों का मौसम होता है

---

[1] शेर का बहुवचन।

Ghazal

It's true! No point in tears and sad despair.
What I demanded from the world is rare.

At dusk the jungle wide, the road unclear.
Just ask me how it seems to me. I'm here.

My rivals have no time to give me pain.
If I'm in need, I find my friends again.

I've seen these wounds with my own eyes today.
But there is balm for them, or so they say!

With verse the branches of the mind abound;
The season of your memory comes round.

मिरे वुजूद[1] से यूँ बेख़बर है वो जैसे
वो एक धूपघड़ी है मैं रात का पल हूँ

---

[1] अस्तित्व ।

She does not even know that I exist, as if
She is a sundial; I, a moment of the night.

ग़ज़ल

शहर के दूकाँदारो! कारोबरे-उलफ़त[1] में
सूद[2] क्या ज़ियाँ[3] क्या है, तुम न जान पाओगे
दिल के दाम कितने हैं ख़्वाब कितने महँगे हैं
और नक़दे-जाँ[4] क्या है तुम न जान पाओगे

कोई कैसे मिलता है फूल कैसे खिलता है
आँख कैसे झुकती है साँस कैसे रुकती है
कैसे रह[5] निकलती है कैसे बात चलती है
शौक़ की ज़बाँ क्या है तुम न जान पाओगे

वस्ल[6] का सुकूँ क्या है हिज्र[7] का जुनूँ[8] क्या है
हुस्न का फ़ुसूँ[9] क्या है इश्क़ के दुरूँ[10] क्या है
तुम मरीज़े-दानाई[11] मस्लहत[12] के शैदाई
राहे गुमरहाँ[13] क्या है तुम न जान पाओगे

ज़ख़्म कैसे फलते हैं दाग़ कैसे जलते हैं
दर्द कैसे होता है, कोई कैसे रोता है
अश्क क्या है नाले[14] क्या दश्त[15] क्या है छाले क्या
आह क्या फुग़ाँ[16] क्या है तुम न जान पाओगे

---

1 दिल का व्यापार; 2 लाभ; 3 हानि; 4 आत्मा की पूँजी; 5 राह; 6 मिलन;
7 विरह; 8 पागलपन; 9 जादू; 10 अंदर; 11 जिसे सोचने-समझने का रोग हो;
12 कूटनीति पसंद करनेवाला; 13 गुमराहों का रास्ता; 14 दर्दभरी आवाज़;
15 वीराना; 16 फ़रियाद।

Ghazal

You, who keep shops in town, selling love for all to buy!
What is profit? What is loss? You will never know.
How expensive are our dreams? Is the price of hearts too high?
And what is the value of soul? You will never know.

How does someone meet another? Flowers bloom, but in what way?
Why does breath stop with a gasp? Why are lovers' eyes cast low?
How to find a way together? How do we know what to say?
In what language do we love? You will never know.

When we meet do we find peace? Is there madness when we part?
What is beauty's magic spell? How does love in secret grow?
You, obsessed by good advice, full of wisdom in your heart,
Where's the path where madmen stray? You will never know.

How are festering wounds produced? Why do scars burn in the heat?
How does anybody weep? How does pain its torment show?
Lamentations, tears and moans; deserts, blisters on the feet?
How are cries from anguish born? You will never know.

नामुराद[1] दिल कैसे सुब्हो-शाम करते हैं
कैसे ज़िंदा रहते हैं और कैसे मरते हैं
तुमको कब नज़र आई ग़मज़दों[2] की तन्हाई
ज़ीस्त बे-अमाँ[3] क्या है तुम न जान पाओगे

जानता हूँ मैं तुमको ज़ौक़े-ए-शाइरी[4] भी है
शख़्सियत[5] सजाने में इक ये माहिरी[6] भी है
फिर भी हर्फ़ चुनते हो सिर्फ़ लफ़्ज़ सुनते हो
इनके दरम्याँ[7] क्या है तुम न जान पाओगे

---

[1] निराश; [2] दुखियारों; [3] असुरक्षित जीवन; [4] शायरी का शौक; [5] व्यक्तित्व; [6] महारत; [7] बीच।

What do aimless wanderers do to pass their days and nights away?
How do they live their wretched lives? Where to die and where to go?
What in grief is loneliness and desolation? Can you say?
What's the point of a restless life? You will never know.

Agreed, you have a taste for verse, a great respect for prosody.
You see it as a social grace, a fine adornment meant for show.
You pick your letters, and you hear the words but only the words.
What's contained between the lines you will never know.

ग़ज़ल

जिस्म दमकता, ज़ुल्फ़ घनेरी, रंगीं लब, आँखें जादू
संग-ए-मरमर, ऊदा बादल, सुर्ख़ शफ़क़[1], हैराँ आहू[2]

भिक्षु दानी, प्यासा पानी, दरिया सागर, जल गागर
गुलशन ख़ुशबू, कोयल कू-कू, मस्ती दारू, मैं और तू

बाँबी नागन, छाया आँगन, घुँघरू छन-छन, आशा मन
आँखें काजल, परबत बादल, वो ज़ुल्फ़ें और ये बाज़ू

रातें महकी, साँसे दहकी, नज़रें बहकी, रुत लहकी
सपन सलोना, प्रेम खिलौना, फूल बिछौना, वो पहलू

तुमसे दूरी, ये मजबूरी, ज़ख़्म-ए-कारी,[3] बेदारी[4]
तनहा रातें, सपने कातें, ख़ुद से बातें मेरी ख़ू[5]

---

[1] लाल क्षितिज; [2] हिरनी; [3] गहरा घाव; [4] जागरण; [5] आदत।

Ghazal

Glowing body, painted lips, magic eyes, curly hair;
Shining marble, scarlet cloud, red horizon, frightened deer.

Alms for beggars, drink for the thirsty, water for the pot,
    river for the sea,
Scent for the garden, song for the cuckoo, wine for the
    drunkard—you and me.

Cobra for the charm-pipe, shade for the yard, tinkling
    bells, hope for the heart,
Eyes with kohl, clouds and hills, your flowing locks, my
    arms apart.

Perfumed nights, burning breath, drunken eyes, rainy weather,
Dreams of beauty, toys of love, scattering flowers, we together.

Parted from you, what can I do? Wounds so deep, sleep
    flies away.
Lonely evenings, weaving dreams, talking to myself—
    that's my way!

उन चराग़ों में तेल ही कम था
क्यों गिला[1] फिर हमें हवा से रहे

---

[1] शिकायत।

My little lamps ran out of oil.
So why complain about the wind?

हिज़[1]

कोई शेर कहूँ
या दुनिया के किसी मौज़ूं[2] पर
मैं कोई नया मज़मून[3] पढ़ूँ
या कोई अनोखी बात सुनूँ
कोई बात
जो हँसनेवाली हो
कोई फ़िक़रा[4]
जो दिलचस्प लगे
या कोई ख़याल अछूता सा
या कहीं मिले
कोई मंज़र
जो हैराँ कर दे
कोई लम्हा
जो दिल को छू जाए
मैं अपने ज़हन के गोशों[5] में
इन सबको सँभाल के रखता हूँ
और सोचता हूँ
जब मिलोगे
तुमको सुनाऊँगा

---

[1] विरह; [2] विषय; [3] लेख; [4] जुमला, वाक्य; [5] कोनों।

Apart

If I compose a verse
Or read of something new,
A subject that concerns the world;
If I hear something uncommon,
Something
That might make you laugh,
A sentence
Which seems interesting,
Or some original idea;
If I am greeted by a sight
Which is stunning,
Some moment
Which touches my heart—
I store all these things
In the recesses of my mind,
And think . . .
That when we meet,
I shall tell them all to you.

मेरी बुनियादों में कोई टेढ़ थी
अपनी दीवारों को क्या इल्ज़ाम दूँ

My foundations went a tiny bit awry,
So why should I be mean and blame my walls?

दुश्वारी[1]

मैं भूल जाऊँ तुम्हें
अब यही मुनासिब है
मगर भुलाना भी चाहूँ तो किस तरह भूलूँ
कि तुम तो फिर भी हक़ीक़त हो
कोई ख़्वाब नहीं
यहाँ तो दिल का ये आलम है क्या कहूँ
कमबख़्त!
भुला न पाया ये वो सिलसिला
जो था ही नहीं
वो इक ख़याल
जो आवाज़ तक गया ही नहीं
वो एक बात
जो मैं कह नहीं सका तुमसे
वो एक रब्त[2]
जो हममें कभी रहा ही नहीं
मुझे है याद वो सब
जो कभी हुआ ही नहीं।

---

[1] कठिनाई; [2] संबंध।

Dilemma

Perhaps I should forget you.
This is now the proper thing to do.
But even if I wish to erase you from my mind,
Then how can I forget?
After all, you are real,
Not just a dream.
That's how I feel.
What can I say?
Damn it!
I could never forget
Those events that never were;
That idea, that one idea
Which was never expressed;
That word, that one word
Which I could not say to you;
That relationship
Which never existed between you and me.
I remember all those things
Which never happened.

तुम्हें भी याद नहीं और मैं भी भूल गया
वो लम्हा कितना हसीं था मगर फुज़ूल[1] गया

---

[1] बेकार।

Even you do not recall, and even I forget
How wonderful that moment, wasted for us yet!

आसार-ए-क़दीमा[1]

एक पत्थर की अधूरी मूरत
चन्द ताँबे के पुराने सिक्के
काली चाँदी के अजब से ज़ेवर
और कई काँसे के टूटे बरतन
एक सहरा में मिले
ज़ेरे-ज़मीं[2]
लोग कहते हैं कि सदियों पहले
आज सहरा है जहाँ
वहीं इक शहर हुआ करता था
और मुझको ये ख़याल आता है
किसी तक़रीब[3]
किसी महफ़िल में
सामना तुझसे मिरा आज भी हो जाता है।
एक लम्हे को
बस इक पल के लिए
जिस्म की आँच
उचटती-सी नज़र
सुर्ख़ बिंदिया की दमक
सरसराहट तिरे मलबूस[4] की
बालों की महक
बेख़याली में कभी

---

[1] भग्नावशेष; [2] ज़मीन के नीचे; [3] समारोह; [4] लिबास।

Remains of the Past

A half-preserved stone statue,
A few old copper coins,
Mysterious jewels of blackened silver,
Some broken plates of brass
Were found in a desert
Under the ground.
People say that centuries ago,
Where the desert stands today,
There used to be a city.
And I imagine
That on some festive occasion,
In some assembly,
I come face to face with you even today.
For a moment,
Just for a second,
The fire of your body,
A fleeting glance,
The rustling of your clothes,
The perfume of your hair,
Sometimes in carelessness,

लम्स[1] का नन्हा-सा फूल
और फिर दूर तक वही सहरा
वही सहरा कि जहाँ
कभी इक शहर हुआ करता था।

The delicate flower of your touch.
And once more that rolling desert,
That desert, where
Once upon a time
A city stood.

ग़ज़ल

फिरते हैं कब से दर-बदर अब इस नगर अब उस नगर
इक दूसरे के हमसफ़र मैं और मिरी अवारगी
नाआश्ना[1] हर रहगुज़र नामेहरबां हर इक नज़र
जाएँ तो अब जाएँ किधर मैं और मिरी अवारगी

हम भी कभी आबाद थे ऐसे कहाँ बरबाद थे
बेफ़िक्र थे आज़ाद थे मसरूर[2] थे दिलशाद[3] थे
वो चाल ऐसी चल गया हम बुझ गए दिल जल गया
निकले जलाके अपना घर मैं और मिरी अवारगी

जीना बहुत आसान था इक शख़्स का एहसान था
हमको भी इक अरमान था जो ख़्वाब का सामान था
अब ख़्वाब हैं न आरज़ू अरमान है न जुस्तजू
यूँ भी चलो खुश हैं मगर मैं और मिरी अवारगी

वो माहवश[4] वो माहरू[5] वो माहे कामिल[6] हू-बहू
थीं जिसकी बातें कू-बकू[7] उससे अजब थी गुफ़्तगू
फिर यूँ हुआ वो खो गयी तो मुझको ज़िद सी हो गई
लाएँगे उसको ढूँढकर मैं और मिरी अवारगी

---

[1] अपरिचित; [2] प्रसन्न; [3] दिल से खुश; [4] चाँद जैसी; [5] चाँद जैसे चेहरे वाली; [6] पूरा चाँद; [7] गली-गली।

Ghazal

From door to door, from town to town, forever passing by,
We are two fellow-travellers, my wandering and I.
With every path unknown to us, and cruel every eye,
Let's take the road, but where to go? My wandering and I.

Once we were settled, never feeling we had gone astray,
Careless, joyful, roaming free, so happy we could fly.
But that is all extinguished now; the heart has lost its flame.
We burnt our house and went away, my wandering and I.

Life was easy, just one person made this gift to us.
The plans we had were made of dreams; we only had to try.
But now there is no dream, no wish, no quest, no plan, no hope.
So let's go on; we're quite content, my wandering and I.

They talked of us in every street; ours was a strange affair;
Her face was like the moon that rises full upon the sky.
But then one day I lost her; and I became obsessed.
We'll look for her and bring her back, my wandering and I.

ये दिल ही था जो सह गया वो बात ऐसी कह गया
कहने को फिर क्या रह गया अश्कों का दरिया बह गया
जब कहके वो दिलबर गया तेरे लिए मैं मर गया
रोते हैं उसको रात भर मैं और मिरी अवारगी

अब ग़म उठाएँ किसलिए आँसू बहाएँ किसलिए
ये दिल जलाएँ किसलिए यूँ जाँ गवाएँ किसलिए
पेशा न हो जिसका सितम ढूँढेंगे अब ऐसा सनम
होंगे कहीं तो कारगर[1] मैं और मिरी अवारगी

आसार हैं सब खोट के इमकान[2] हैं सब चोट के
घर बंद हैं सब गोट के अब ख़त्म हैं सब टोटके
क़िस्मत का सब ये फेर है अँधेर है अँधेर है
ऐसे हुए हैं बेअसर मैं और मिरी अवारगी

जब हमदमो हमराज़ था तब और ही अंदाज़ था
अब सोज़[3] है तब साज़[4] था अब शर्म है तब नाज़ था
अब मुझसे हो तो भी क्या है साथ वो तो वो भी क्या
इक बेहुनर[5] इक बेसमर[6] मैं और मिरी अवारगी

My heart became resigned, and then she said such things to me,
And what she said just left me with a sea of tears to cry.
My sweetheart left me with these words: 'Now I am dead for you!'
We weep for her the whole night long, my wandering and I.

Now why should we put up with grief, and why should we shed tears?
And why should we destroy our life, and burn our hearts and sigh?
We'll find another, who does not make cruelty her trade;
We'll be successful somewhere else, my wandering and I.

There's every sign of faithlessness, all means to suffer pain;
The pawn cannot manoeuvre, and all spells have proved a lie.
Misfortune comes at every turn, injustice all around.
So ineffectual we have been, my wandering and I.

So different when a friend would share the secrets of our heart.
Now pain replaces joy, and pride falls with a shameful cry.
Can we accomplish anything, though we walk side by side?
One fruitless, one useless, my wandering and I.

ग़म बिकते हैं

ग़म बिकते हैं
बाज़ारों में
ग़म काफ़ी महँगे बिकते हैं
लहजे की दुक्कान अगर चल जाए तो
जज़्बे[1] के गाहक
छोटे बड़े हर ग़म के खिलौने
मुँह माँगी क़ीमत पे ख़रीदें
मैंने हमेशा अपने ग़म अच्छे दामों बेचे हैं
लेकिन
जो ग़म मुझको आज मिला है
किसी दुकाँ पर रखने के क़ाबिल ही नहीं है
पहली बार मैं शर्मिन्दा हूँ
ये ग़म बेच नही पाऊँगा।

---

[1] भावनाओं।

Sorrows for Sale

Sorrows are sold
In the market.
The price of sorrows is high.
If the shop of sweet tones is successful,
The customers of emotion
Will buy the toys of sorrow, large or small,
For any price that is asked.
I have always
Sold my sorrows for a good price
But
The sorrow I have today
I could not display it on any counter.
For the first time I am ashamed;
This sorrow I shall not be able to sell.

थकन से चूर पास आया था इसके
गिरा सोते में मुझ पर ये शजर[1] क्यों

---

[1] पेड़।

Tired out, exhausted, I drew near this tree.
Why did it fall on me in my sleep?

आओ, और न सोचो

आओ
और न सोचो
सोच के क्या पाओगे
जितना भी समझे हो
उतना पछताए हो
जितना भी समझोगे
उतना पछताओगे
आओ
और न सोचो
सोच के क्या पाओगे

तुम एहसास की जिस मंज़िल पर अब पहुँचे हो
वो मेरी देखी-भाली है
जाने भी दो
इसका कब तक सोग मनाना
ये दुनिया
अंदर से इतनी क्यूँ काली है
आओ
कुछ अब जीने का सामान करें हम
सच के हाथों
हमने जो मुश्किल पाई है
झूठ के हाथों
वो मुश्किल आसान करें हम

Come Now and Do Not Think

Come now
And do not think.
What will you gain by thinking?
All that you have understood
You have regretted.
All that you will understand
You will regret.
Come now
And do not think.
What will you gain from thinking?

The level of feeling you have now attained,
This is in my care.
Forget that as well.
How long will you grieve for it?
Why is this world
So vile on the inside?
Come now
Let us find some way to live.
The problems given us by truth,
Let us make them easier
With lies.

तुम मेरी आँखों में आँखे डालके देखो
फिर मैं तुमसे
सारी झूठी क़समें खाऊँ
फिर तुम वो सारी झूठी बातें दोहराओ
जो सबको अच्छी लगती हैं
जैसे
वफ़ा करने की बातें
जीने की मरने की बातें
हम दोनों
यूँ वक़्त गुज़ारें
मैं तुमको कुछ ख़्वाब दिखाऊँ
तुम मुझको कुछ ख़्वाब दिखाओ
जिनकी
कोई ताबीर[1] नहीं हो
जितने दिन ये मेल रहेगा
देखो अच्छा खेल रहेगा
और
कभी दिल भर जाए तो
कह देना तुम
बीत गया मिलने का मौसम

आओ
और न सोचो
सोच के क्या पाओगे

---

[1] सपने का अर्थ।

Look at me. Look into my eyes.
Then I shall swear to you all my false oaths;
And you will repeat all those false words,
Which everybody loves,
Like
Protestations that we would
Live and die together.
Let us, you and I together,
Spend our time in this way.
I'll show you some dreams.
Then you can show me some dreams,
Which
Have no interpretation.
And as long as we meet,
Oh, the game will be sweet!
And when you become disenchanted,
Tell me:
'The time of our meeting is over.'

Come now
And do not think.
What will you gain by thinking?

उनसे अब वापस ख़रीदूँ ख़ुद को मैं
लोग जो माँगें वो अपने दाम दूँ

I sold myself. I'll ask to have it back.
And give whatever price the vendor asks!

ग़ज़ल

मेरे दिल में उतर गया सूरज
तीरगी[1] में निखर गया सूरज

दर्स[2] देकर हमें उजाले का
ख़ुद अँधेरे के घर गया सूरज

हमसे वादा था इक सवेरे का
हाय कैसा मुकर गया सूरज

चाँदनी अक्स, चाँद आईना
आईने में सँवर गया सूरज

डूबते वक़्त ज़र्द[3] था इतना
लोग समझे कि मर गया सूरज

---

[1] अँधेरा; [2] शिक्षा; [3] पीला।

Ghazal

In my heart it set—the sun
So bright in gloom became the sun.

It taught us all we know of light,
And then in darkness plunged the sun.

It promised us an early dawn.
Alas that we believed the sun!

Moonlight reflection; moon the mirror;
In the mirror how fair the sun.

And when it sank, it looked so pale,
And all began to mourn the sun.

एक खिलौना जोगी से खो गया था बचपन में
ढूँढता फिरा उसको वो नगर-नगर तनहा

In childhood once a yogi lost his toy
And searched for it from town to town alone.

वक़्त

ये वक़्त क्या है
ये क्या है आख़िर कि जो मुसलसल[1] गुज़र रहा है
ये जब न गुज़रा था
तब कहाँ था
कहीं तो होगा
गुज़र गया है
तो अब कहाँ है
कहीं तो होगा
कहाँ से आया किधर गया है
ये कब से कब तक का सिलसिला है
ये वक़्त क्या है

वे वाक़ए[2]
हादसे[3]
तसादुम[4]
हर एक ग़म
और हर इक मसर्रत[5]
हर इक अज़ीयत[6]
हर एक लज़्ज़त[7]
हर एक तबस्सुम[8]

---

[1] लगातार; [2] घटनाएँ; [3] दुर्घटनाएँ; [4] टकराव; [5] खुशी; [6] तकलीफ़; [7] आनंद;
[8] मुस्कान ।

Time

What is time?
What is this thing that goes on without pause?
If it did not pass,
Then where could it have been?
It must have been somewhere.
It has passed.
So where is it now?
It must be somewhere.
Where did it come from? Where did it go?
Where did the process start? Where will it end?
What is time?

These events
Incidents
Conflicts
Every grief
Every joy
Every torment
Every pleasure
Every smile

हर एक आँसू
हर एक नग़मा[1]
हर एक ख़ुशबू
वो ज़ख़्म का दर्द हो
कि वो लम्स[2] का हो जादू
ख़ुद अपनी आवाज़ हो कि माहौल की सदाएँ[3]
ये ज़हन में बनती और बिगड़ती हुई फ़िज़ाएँ
वो फ़िक्र में आए ज़लज़ले[4] हों
कि दिल की हलचल
तमाम एहसास
सारे जज़्बे
ये जैसे पत्ते हैं
बहते पानी की सतह पर
जैसे तैरते हैं
अभी यहाँ हैं
अभी वहाँ हैं
और अब हैं ओझल
दिखाई देता नहीं है लेकिन
ये कुछ तो है
जो कि बह रहा है
ये कैसा दरिया है
किन पहाड़ों से आ रहा है
ये किस समंदर को जा रहा है
ये वक़्त क्या है

---

[1] गीत; [2] स्पर्श; [3] आवाज़ें; [4] भूचाल।

Every tear

Every song

Every scent.

It may be the pain of a wound

Or the magic of a tender touch,

One lonely voice or cries around;

Successes and failures assailing the mind;

The upheavals of care, the tumult of the heart.

All feelings

All emotions

Are like leaves

Floating on the surface of the water.

As they swim along

Now here,

Now there,

And now they disappear,

Gone from sight, but

There must be something

Flowing along.

What is this river?

What hills has it come from?

To what sea is it going?

What is time?

कभी कभी मैं ये सोचता हूँ
कि चलती गाड़ी से पेड़ देखो
तो ऐसा लगता है
दूसरी सम्त[1] जा रहे हैं
मगर हक़ीक़त में
पेड़ अपनी जगह खड़े हैं
तो क्या ये मुमकिन है
सारी सदियाँ
क़तार अंदर क़तार[2] अपनी जगह खड़ी हों
ये वक़्त साकित[3] हो
और हम ही गुज़र रहे हों
इस एक लम्हे में
सारे लम्हे
तमाम सदियाँ छुपी हुई हों
न कोई आइंदा[4]
न गुज़िश्ता[5]
जो हो चुका है
वो हो रहा है
जो होनेवाला है
हो रहा है
मैं सोचता हूँ
कि क्या ये मुमकिन है
सच ये हो
कि सफ़र में हम हैं

---

[1] दिशा; [2] पंक्ति दर पंक्ति; [3] ठहरा हुआ; [4] भविष्य; [5] भूतकाल।

Sometimes I think
When I see trees from a moving train,
It seems
They go in the opposite way.
But in reality
The trees are standing still.
So can it be
That all our centuries,
Row upon row, are standing still?
Can it be that time is fixed,
And we alone are in motion?
Can it be that in this one moment
All moments,
All centuries are hidden?
No future
No past.
What has gone by
Is happening now.
What will come about
Is happening now.
I think—
Can it be possible
That this is true,
That we are in motion?

गुज़रते हम हैं
जिसे समझते हैं हम
गुज़रता है
वो थमा है
गुज़रता है या थमा हुआ है
इकाई है या बँटा हुआ है
है मुंजमिद[1]
या पिघल रहा है
किसे ख़बर है
किसे पता है
ये वक़्त क्या है

ये क़ाएनाते-अज़ीम[2]
लगता है
अपनी अज़मत[3] से
आज भी मुतमइन[4] नहीं है
कि लम्हा–लम्हा
वसीइतर[5] और वसीइतर होती जा रही है
ये अपनी बाँहें पसारती है
ये कहकशाँओं[6] की उँगलियों से
नये ख़लाओं[7] को छू रही है
अगर ये सच है
तो हर तसव्वुर[8] की हद से बाहर

---

[1] जमा हुआ; [2] विशाल ब्रह्मांड; [3] महानता; [4] संतुष्ट; [5] विशाल; [6] आकाशगंगाओं; [7] अंतरिक्षों; [8] कल्पना।

We pass by,
And what we imagine
Is moving
Is really motionless.
Moving, not moving?
Whole or divided?
Is it frozen,
Or is it melting?
Who knows?
Who can guess?
What is time?

This glorious universe
It seems
Even today is not content
With all its glory.
At every moment
It becomes wider and more vast.
It stretches out its arms
And with its fingers like galaxies
Touches other parts of space.
If this is true,
Outside the bounds of all we can imagine

मगर कहीं पर
यक़ीनन[1] ऐसा कोई ख़ला है
कि जिसको
इन कहकशाँओं की उँगलियों ने
अब तक छुआ नहीं है
ख़ला
जहाँ कुछ हुआ नहीं है
ख़ला
कि जिसने किसी से भी 'कुन'[2] सुना नहीं है
जहाँ अभी तक ख़ुदा नहीं है
वहाँ
कोई वक़्त भी न होगा
ये क़ाएनाते-अज़ीम
इक दिन
छुएगी
उस अनछुए ख़ला को
और अपने सारे वुजूद[3] से
जब पुकारेगी
'कुन'
तो वक़्त को भी जनम मिलेगा
अगर जनम है तो मौत भी है
मैं सोचता हूँ
ये सच नहीं है
कि वक़्त की कोई इब्तिदा[4] है न इन्तहा[5] है

---

1 निस्संदेह; 2 'हो जा' माना जाता है कि ईश्वर के इन शब्दों से सृष्टि
की रचना हुई थी; 3 अस्तित्व; 4 आदि; 5 अंत।

Somewhere there will certainly be a part of space,
Which
So far it has not touched
With its fingers like galaxies,
Where nothing has happened.
A part of space,
Which has not heard the Creator's command,
'Be!'
Where God does not yet exist.
And in that place
There will be no time
One day
This glorious universe will reach
This untouched part of space.
And then with its whole existence
It will cry:
'Be!'
Time will be born there also.
If there is birth, then there is death.
I think
It is not true
That time has no end and no beginning.

ये डोर लंबी बहुत है
लेकिन
कहीं तो इस डोर का सिरा है
अभी ये इनसाँ उलझ रहा है
कि वक़्त के इस क़फ़स[1] में पैदा हुआ
यहीं वो पला-बढ़ा है
मगर उसे इल्म[2] हो गया है
कि वक़्त के इस क़फ़स से बाहर भी
इक फ़िज़ा[3] है
तो सोचता है
वो पूछता है
ये वक़्त क्या है?

---

[1] पिंजरे; [2] ज्ञान; [3] वातावरण।

The thread is very long
But
Somewhere the thread will have an end.
Now mankind is confused
Because it was born in this cage of time.
It was brought up and raised here.
But now man has discovered
That outside the cage of time
There lies another part of space.
So he thinks,
He asks,
What is time?

ग़ज़ल

दर्द के फूल भी खिलते हैं बिखर जाते हैं
ज़ख़्म कैसे भी हों कुछ रोज़ में भर जाते हैं

रास्ता रोके खड़ी है यही उलझन कब से
कोई पूछे तो कहें क्या कि किधर जाते हैं

छत की कड़ियों से उतरते हैं मिरे ख़्वाब मगर
मेरी दीवारों से टकरा के बिखर जाते हैं

नर्म अल्फ़ाज़[1], भली बातें, मुहज़्ज़ब[2] लहजे
पहली बारिश ही में ये रंग उतर जाते हैं

उस दरीचे[3] में भी अब कोई नहीं और हम भी
सर झुकाये हुए चुपचाप गुज़र जाते हैं

---

[1] शब्द; [2] सभ्य बोली; [3] खिड़की।

Ghazal

Once blown the flowers of pain are scattered on the field.
However bad our wounds may be, at last they're healed.

How long has this confusion blocked my way?
If someone asks me where I go, what shall I say?

And from the beams of my old roof my dreams descend.
They crash against the walls and shatter in the end.

Soft words and cultured conversation, talk in vain!
These colours fade as soon as it begins to rain.

There's no one waiting by the window now, and I,
With silent steps and head so humbly bowed, pass by.

आगही[1] से मिली है तनहाई
आ मिरी जान मुझको धोखा दे

204

From knowing you I suffered loneliness;
So come, my dear! Time to deceive me now.

ग़ज़ल

मुझको यक़ीं है सच कहती थीं जो भी अम्मी कहती थीं
जब मेरे बचपन के दिन थे चाँद में परियाँ रहती थीं

एक ये दिन जब अपनों ने भी हमसे नाता तोड़ लिया
एक वो दिन जब पेड़ की शाख़ें बोझ हमारा सहती थीं

एक ये दिन जब सारी सड़कें रूठी-रूठी लगती हैं
एक वो दिन जब 'आओ खेलें' सारी गलियाँ कहती थीं

एक ये दिन जब जागी रातें दीवारों को तकती हैं
एक वो दिन जब शामों की भी पलकें बोझिल रहती थीं

एक ये दिन जब ज़हन में सारी अय्यारी[1] की बातें हैं
एक वो दिन जब दिल में भोली-भाली बातें रहती थीं

एक ये दिन जब लाखों ग़म और काल पड़ा है आँसू का
एक वो दिन जब एक ज़रा सी बात पे नदियाँ बहती थीं

एक ये घर जिस घर में मेरा साज़ों-सामाँ[2] रहता है
एक वो घर जिस घर में मेरी बूढ़ी नानी रहती थीं

---

[1] चालाकी; [2] तामझाम।

206

Ghazal

My mother was quite right, and I believe it all;
The fairies lived upon the moon when I was small.

This is the day when my own people break with me,
But once the boughs would bear my weight so easily.

This is the day when streets are eager for the fray,
But once the streets would gaily shout: 'Come out to play!'

This is the day when sleepless nights stare at the wall.
But once at evening heavy eyelids used to fall.

This is the day when cunning thoughts beset my mind,
But once my heart had simple thoughts, and they were kind.

This is the day when grief abounds and tears are done,
But once, for nothing, tears could make a river run.

This is a house with everything on every side;
That was the house where my grandmother lived and died.

दोराहा

अपनी बेटी ज़ोया के नाम

ये जीवन इक राह नहीं
इक दोराहा है

पहला रस्ता
बहुत सहल है
इसमें कोई मोड़ नहीं है
ये रस्ता
इस दुनिया से बेजोड़ नहीं है
इस रस्ते पर मिलते हैं
रीतों के आँगन
इस रस्ते पर मिलते हैं
रिश्तों के बंधन
इस रस्ते पर चलनेवाले
कहने को सब सुख पाते हैं
लेकिन
टुकड़े टुकड़े होकर
सब रिश्तों में बँट जाते हैं
अपने पल्ले कुछ नहीं बचता
बचती है
बेनाम सी उलझन
बचता है
साँसों का ईंधन

Crossroads

For my daughter Zoya

Life is not a road,
Life is a crossroads.

The first path is very easy,
It has no turn.
This path
Is not separate from the world.
On this path you find
Courtyards of rules.
On this path you find
Bonds of relationships.
But those who tread this path
Find all their pleasures in name alone.
They fall to pieces
And are divided amongst all those ties.
Nothing is left for them.
All that is left
Is confusion without name.
All that is left
Is fuel of the breath.

जिसमें उनकी अपनी हर पहचान
और उनके सारे सपने
जल बुझते हैं
इस रस्ते पर चलनेवाले
खुद को खोकर जग पाते हैं
ऊपर-ऊपर तो जीते हैं
अंदर-अंदर मर जाते हैं।

दूसरा रस्ता
बहुत कठिन है
इस रस्ते में
कोई किसी के साथ नहीं है
कोई सहारा देनेवाला हाथ नहीं है
इस रस्ते में धूप है
कोई छाँव नहीं है
जहाँ तसल्ली भीख में देदे कोई किसी को
इस रस्ते में
ऐसा कोई गाँव नहीं है
ये उन लोगों का रस्ता है
जो खुद अपने तक जाते हैं
अपने आपको जो पाते हैं
तुम इस रस्ते पर ही चलना।

मुझे पता है
ये रस्ता आसान नहीं है
लेकिन मुझको ये ग़म भी है

In which their sense of self and
All their dreams burn and go out.
Those who take this path
Lose themelves to please the world
On the surface they live;
Inside they die.

The second path
Is very hard.
On this path
No one goes with another.
No one lends a hand to give support.
On this path
There is scorching sun;
There is no shade
Where one consoles another with charity.
On this path
There is no such village.
This is the path of those
Who travel towards themselves,
Who discover their own true self.
Take this path.

I know
This path is not easy.
But one thing saddens me:

तुमको अब तक
क्यूँ अपनी पहचान नहीं है।

So far
You have not found yourself.

रात सर पर है और सफ़र बाक़ी
हमको चलना ज़रा सवेरे था।

The night draws in; we have so far to go.
We should have started earlier today.

ग़ज़ल

मिरी ज़िंदगी, मिरी मंज़िलें, मुझे कुर्ब[1] में नहीं, दूर दे
मुझे तू दिखा वही रास्ता, जो सफ़र के बाद ग़ुरूर[2] दे

वही जज़्बा दे जो शदीद[3] हो, हो ख़ुशी तो जैसे कि ईद हो
कभी ग़म मिले तो बला का हो, मुझे वो भी एक सुरूर[4] दे

तू ग़लत न समझे तो मैं कहूँ, तिरा शुक्रिया कि दिया सुकूँ[5]
जो बढ़े तो बढ़के बने जुनूँ, मुझे वो ख़लिश[6] भी ज़रूर दे

मुझे तूने की है अता[7] ज़बाँ, मुझे ग़म सुनाने का ग़म कहाँ
रहे अनकही मिरी दास्ताँ, मुझे नुत्क़[8] पर वो उबूर[9] दे

ये जो ज़ुल्फ़ तेरी उलझ गई, वो जो थी कभी तिरी धज गई
मैं तुझे सवारूँगा ज़िंदगी, मिरे हाथ में ये उमूर[10] दे

---

[1] पास; [2] अभिमान; [3] तीव्र; [4] नशा; [5] शांति; [6] टीस; [7] वरदान; [8] बोलने की शक्ति; [9] कौशलता; [10] कार्य।

Ghazal

Oh life! Give me those distant goals that take me far and wide.
Show me a road, a winding path, which will afford me pride.

Let me have strong emotions; give me pleasure in excess.
If grief becomes disaster, that will be my happiness.

You gave me peace. If I should thank you for it do not fret.
But make me writhe; let pain increase and turn to madness yet.

The tongue you gave me for expressing grief is far too bold.
Give me the power to check it. Let my tale remain untold.

Your hair is tangled and the looks you had no longer flower.
But I can rearrange you, my dear life; I have that power.

सब हवाएँ ले गया मेरे समंदर की कोई
और मुझको एक कश्ती बादबानी[1] दे गया

---

[1] पालवाली नाव।

Someone robbed my sea of wind,
And left me with a sailing boat.

ग़ज़ल

किन लफ़्ज़ों में इतनी कड़वी इतनी कसीली बात लिखूँ
शे'र की मैं तहज़ीब[1] निबाहूँ या अपने हालात लिखूँ

ग़म नहीं लिक्खूँ क्या मैं ग़म को जश्न लिखूँ क्या मातम को
जो देखे हैं मैंने जनाज़े क्या उनको बारात लिखूँ

कैसे लिखूँ मैं चाँद के क़िस्से कैसे लिखूँ मैं फूल की बात
रेत उड़ाए गर्म हवा तो कैसे मैं बरसात लिखूँ

किस किस की आँखों में देखे मैंने ज़हर बुझे ख़ंजर
ख़ुद से भी जो मैने छुपाए कैसे वो सदमात[2] लिखूँ

तख़्त की ख़्वाहिश, लूट की लालच, कमज़ोरों पर जुल्म का शौक़
लेकिन उनका फ़रमाना है मैं इनको जज़्बात लिखूँ

क़ातिल भी मक़तूल[3] भी दोनों नाम ख़ुदा का लेते थे
कोई ख़ुदा है तो वो कहाँ था मेरी क्या औक़ात[4] लिखूँ

अपनी अपनी तारीकी[5] को लोग उजाला कहते हैं
तारीकी के नाम लिखूँ तो क़ौमें, फ़िरक़े[6], ज़ात लिखूँ

---

[1] परंपरा; [2] सदमे का बहुवचन; [3] जिसकी हत्या हुई; [4] हैसियत; [5] अंधकार;
[6] वर्ग।

Ghazal

This suffering, this bitterness, what words can best reveal?
Shall I adopt the norm of verse or write the way I feel?

Grief and tears are not for pleasure; that I'll say at least.
Shall I describe a funeral pyre like a wedding feast?

I should write stories of the moon and flowers; that is plain,
But if the wind throws sand at me, then shall I talk of rain?

Daggers dipped in poison I have seen in people's eyes.
Shall I describe the cruelty that I myself disguise?

They want to rule and plunder, and oppress the helpless too;
'Just call them mere emotions.' That is what I'm told to do.

The murderer and the victim take the name of God in vain.
If God exists, then where was He? Shall I lament my pain?

Most people call their darkness light. But when I write at last
Of darkness, shall I make my subject nation, sect and caste?

जाने ये कैसा दौर है जिसमें ये जुरअत[1] भी मुश्किल है
दिन हो अगर तो उसको लिखूँ दिन, रात अगर हो रात लिखूँ

---

[1] हिम्मत।

In this age, why so difficult to put down what is right?
Can't I declare that day is day, and say that night is night?

सुबह की गोरी

रात की काली चादर ओढ़े
मुँह को लपेटे
सोई है कब से
रूठ के सबसे
सुबह की गोरी
आँख न खोले
मुँह से न बोले
जब से किसी ने
कर ली है सूरज की चोरी

आओ
चल के सूरज ढूँढें
और न मिले तो
किरन किरन फिर जमा करें हम
और इक सूरज नया बनाएँ
सोई है कब से
रूठ के सबसे
सुबह की गोरी
उसे जगाएँ
उसे मनाएँ

Morning Maiden

Wrapping herself in night's black mantle,
Hiding her face,
The morning maiden
Fast asleep
She will not peep
From under her shawl
Or say a word.
She's vexed with all
Since someone stole
The sun away.

Come
Let's find the sun for her.
And if we don't we'll gather rays
And make a new one.
So long she sleeps
And pouts and weeps.
Let us wake her,
Let us make her
Happy.

मेरी दुआ है

ख़ला[1] के गहरे समंदरों में
अगर कहीं कोई है जज़ीरा[2]
जहाँ कोई साँस ले रहा है
जहाँ कोई दिल धड़क रहा है
जहाँ ज़हानत[3] ने इल्म[4] का जाम पी लिया है
जहाँ के बासी
ख़ला के गहरे समंदरों में
उतारने को हैं अपने बेड़े
तलाश करने कोई जज़ीरा
जहाँ कोई साँस ले रहा है
जहाँ कोई दिल धड़क रहा है

मेरी दुआ है
कि उस जज़ीरे में रहनेवालों के जिस्म का रंग
इस जज़ीरे के रहनेवालों के जिस्म के जितने रंग हैं
उनसे मुख़्तलिफ़[5] हो
बदन की हैअत[6] भी मुख़्तलिफ़
और शक्लोसूरत भी मुख़्तलिफ़ हो

मिरी दुआ है
अगर है उनका भी कोई मज़हब

---

[1] अंतरिक्ष; [2] द्वीप; [3] बुद्धिमत्ता; [4] ज्ञान; [5] भिन्न; [6] रूप।

My Prayer

In the deep oceans of space
If somewhere there is an island
Where someone is breathing
Where some heart is beating
Where intelligence has drunk from the cup of knowledge,
Those who dwell there
Will come over the deep oceans of space
And moor their ships
And discover some other island
Where someone is breathing
Where some heart is beating.

It is my prayer
That the colour of the bodies
Of those who dwell on that island,
Should be different from the colours of the bodies
Of the inhabitants of this island;
The shape of their bodies should be different from ours
Their form and looks should be different from ours.

It is my prayer
That if they have a religion

तो इस जज़ीरे के मज़हबों से वो मुख़्तलिफ़ हो
मिरी दुआ है
कि इस जज़ीरे की सब ज़बानों से मुख़्तलिफ़ हो
ज़बान उनकी

मिरी दुआ है
ख़ला के गहरे समंदरों से गुज़र के
इक दिन
उस अजनबी नस्ल के जहाज़ी
ख़लाई[1] बेड़े में
इस जज़ीरे तक आएँ
हम उनके मेज़बाँ[2] हों
हम उनको हैरत से देखते हों
वो पास आकर
हमें इशारों से ये बतायें
कि उनसे हम इतने मुख़्तलिफ़ हैं
कि उनको लगता है
इस जज़ीरे के रहनेवाले
सब एक से हैं

मिरी दुआ है
कि इस जज़ीरे के रहनेवाले
उस अजनबी नस्ल के कहे का यक़ीन कर लें।

---

[1] अंतरिक्ष के जहाज़ों; [2] मेहमान का सत्कार करनेवाले।

Then it should be different
From the religion of this island.
It is my prayer
That their language should be different
From all the tongues of this island.

It is my prayer
That, having crossed the deep oceans of space,
One day
The mariners of that strange race
In their cosmic fleet
Should come to this island.
And we shall be their hosts.
We shall look at them in amazement.
They will come to us
And tell us in signs
That we look so different from them
But it seems to them
That the dwellers of our island
All look the same.

It is my prayer
That the dwellers of this island
Will believe what the strange race says.

पहले भी कुछ लोगों ने जौ बो कर गेहूँ चाहा था
हम भी इस उम्मीद में हैं लेकिन कब ऐसा होता है

Once people planted barley and they wanted wheat.
I also hope for that but find it does not work.

ग़ज़ल

दुख के जंगल में फिरते हैं कब से मारे मारे लोग
जो होता है सह लेते हैं कैसे हैं बेचारे लोग

जीवन-जीवन हमने जग में खेल यही होते देखा
धीरे-धीरे जीती दुनिया धीरे-धीरे हारे लोग

वक़्त सिंहासन पर बैठा है अपने राग सुनाता है
संगत देने को पाते हैं साँसों के इकतारे लोग

नेकी इक दिन काम आती है हमको क्या समझाते हो
हमने बेबस मरते देखे कैसे प्यारे-प्यारे लोग

इस नगरी में क्यों मिलती है रोटी सपनों के बदले
जिनकी नगरी है वो जानें हम ठहरे बँजारे लोग

Ghazal

How long have people wandered in the jungle of the night!
They take the pain that they are dealt and bear their sorry plight.

From life to life throughout the world we go as fate may choose;
The world revolves and slowly wins, and slowly people lose.

And Time sits on its throne and sings its song of victory;
And people's voices crown its instrument with harmony.

'Goodness brings its own reward.' This promise is a lie!
I have seen such fine, good people ruined when they die.

In this town, why, for the price of dreams, are people given bread?
The people of this town may know. The gypsy path we tread.

मेरे कुछ पल मुझको दे दो बाकी सारे दिन लोगो
तुम जैसा जैसा कहते हो सब वैसा वैसा होगा

I ask for a few of my moments;
All my days I do not demand.
Whatever you say, oh people,
Will be done as you command.

ग़ज़ल

बहाना ढूँढते रहते हैं कोई रोने का
हमें ये शौक़ है क्या आस्तीं भिगोने का

अगर पलक पे है मोती तो ये नहीं काफ़ी
हुनर भी चाहिए अल्फ़ाज़[1] में पिरोने का

जो फ़स्ल ख़्वाब की तैयार है तो ये जानो
कि वक़्त आ गया फिर दर्द कोई बोने का

ये ज़िंदगी भी अजब कारोबार है कि मुझे
खुशी है पाने की कोई न रंज खोने का

है पाश-पाश[2] मगर फिर भी मुस्कुराता है
वो चेहरा जैसे हो टूटे हुए खिलौने का

---

[1] शब्द; [2] चकनाचूर।

Ghazal

We look for an excuse to weep and grieve.
Why do we always love to wet our sleeve?

How fine the pearl upon the eyelash! Still
To thread it into words you need the skill.

If dreams are ready for the harvest, know
The time of pain has come. Prepare to sow.

This life is a strange business when I see
That gain and loss are all the same to me.

Someone is shattered with grief, still smiles with joy.
Just like the face upon a broken toy.

जुर्म और सज़ा

हाँ गुनहगार हूँ मैं
जो सज़ा चाहे अदालत देदे
आपके सामने सरकार हूँ मैं

मुझको इक़रार[1]
कि मैंने इक दिन
ख़ुद को नीलाम किया
और राज़ी-बरज़ा[2]
सरेबाज़ार, सरेआम किया
मुझको क़ीमत भी बहुत ख़ूब मिली थी लेकिन
मैंने सौदे में ख़यानत[3] कर ली
यानी
कुछ ख़्वाब बचाकर रक्खे
मैंने सोचा था
किसे फ़ुरसत है
जो मिरी रूह, मिरे दिल की तलाशी लेगा
मैंने सोचा था
किसे होगी ख़बर
कितना नादान था मैं
ख़्वाब
छुप सकते हैं क्या

---

[1] स्वीकार; [2] अपनी मर्ज़ी से; [3] बेईमानी।

Crime and Punishment

Yes, I am a sinner.
Let the court punish me accordingly.
I stand before you.

I confess
That one day
I put myself up for auction,
And of my own free will
In the marketplace I made it public.
I even obtained a good price
But I was dishonest in my trading.
I mean
I kept a few dreams back.
I thought
Who has the time
To search my soul and my heart
I thought
Who will know?
How naïve I was!
Can dreams be hidden?

रौशनी
मुट्ठी में रुक सकती है क्या
वो जो होना था
हुआ
आपके सामने सरकार हूँ मैं
जो सज़ा चाहे अदालत देदे
फ़ैसला सुनने को तैयार हूँ मैं
हाँ गुनहगार हूँ मैं

फ़ैसला ये है अदालत का
तिरे सारे ख़्वाब
आज से तिरे नहीं हैं मुजरिम!
ज़हन के सारे सफ़र
और तिरे दिल की परवाज़[1]
जिस्म में बहते लहू के नग़मे
रूह का साज़
समाअत[2]
आवाज़
आज से तेरे नहीं हैं मुजरिम!
वस्ल[3] की सारी हदीसें[4]
ग़मे हिज्राँ[5] की किताब
तेरी यादों के गुलाब
तेरा एहसास
तिरी फ़िक्रो नज़र[6]

---

[1] उड़ान; [2] सुनने की शक्ति; [3] मिलन; [4] पवित्र वर्णन; [5] विरह के दुख; [6] वैचारिक दृष्टि।

Can light

Be concealed in a clenched fist.

The inevitable came about.

I stand before you.

Let the court punish me accordingly.

I am prepared for your decision.

Yes, I have sinned.

The court reached its decision:

'All your dreams

Are no longer your property, Criminal!

All the journeys of your fancy,

The flight of your heart,

The songs of the blood flowing through your body,

The instruments of your soul,

The power of hearing, your voice

Are no longer your property, Criminal!

The tales of lovers' meeting,

The book of separation's sorrow,

The flowers of your memories,

Your feelings,

All that you think and see,

तेरी सब साअतें[1]
सब लम्हे तिरे
रोज़ो-शब, शामो-सहर[2]
आज से तेरे नहीं हैं मुजरिम!
ये तो इन्साफ़ हुआ तेरे ख़रीदारों से
और अब तेरी सज़ा
तुझे मरने की इजाज़त नहीं
जीना होगा।

---

[1] क्षण; [2] रात दिन, शाम सवेरे।

All your moments,

Night and day, evening and morning

Are no longer your property, Criminal!

Those who bought from you now have their justice.

And now the punishment:

You are not allowed to die.

You are condemned to live!'

हिल-स्टेशन

घुल रहा है सारा मंज़र शाम धुँधली हो गई
चाँदनी की चादर ओढ़े हर पहाड़ी सो गई

वादियों में पेड़ हैं अब नीलगूँ[1] परछाइयाँ
उठ रहा है कोहरा जैसे चाँदनी का हो धुआँ

चाँद पिघला तो चटानें भी मुलायम हो गयीं
रात की साँसें जो महकीं और मद्धम हो गईं

नर्म है जितनी हवा उतनी फ़िज़ा ख़ामोश है
टहनियों पर ओस पी के हर कली बेहोश है

मोड़ पर करवट लिए अब ऊँघते हैं रास्ते
दूर कोई गा रहा है जाने किसके वास्ते

ये सुकूँ[2] में खोई वादी नूर[3] की जागीर है
दूधिया पर्दे के पीछे सुरमई तस्वीर है

धुल गई है रूह लेकिन दिल को ये एहसास है
ये सूकूँ बस चन्द लमहों को ही मेरे पास है

---

[1] नीले रंग की; [2] शांति; [3] पवित्र उजाला।

Hill Station

The vista fades in evening mist, and every hill
Sleeps gently in a sheet of moonbeams, calm and still.

The trees are blue reflections in the tinted vale;
The haze is rising like the smoke of moonlight pale.

The moon has melted; rocks grow softer in its light
And perfume, even softer, scents the breath of night.

The sky as silent as the breeze of dusk is calm;
The buds are drunk; the branches gave them heady balm.

The road in sleep turns over, bending, winding, slow.
And someone sings a song. For whom? We'll never know.

In heaven's light the valley basks and peace prevails,
A picture of black-tinted eyes through milky veils.

My soul is cleansed, my heart is captured with a song.
But then I know the peace I have will not last long.

फ़ासलों की गर्द में ये सादगी खो जाएगी
शहर जाकर ज़िंदगी फिर शहर की हो जाएगी

This innocence will go to distance, dust and strife.
The city will reclaim me with its city life!

चार क़तए

कत्थई आँखों वाली इक लडकी
एक ही बात पर बिगड़ती है
तुम मुझे क्यों नहीं मिले पहले
रोज़ ये कह के मुझ से लड़ती है

लाख हों हम में प्यार की बातें
ये लड़ाई हमेशा चलती है
उसके इक दोस्त से मैं जलता हूँ
मेरी इक दोस्त से वो जलती है

पास आकर भी फ़ासले क्यों हैं
राज क्या है समझ में ये आया
उस को भी याद है कोई अब तक
मैं भी तुमको भुला नहीं पाया

हम भी काफी तेज़ थे पहले
वो भी थी अय्यार[1] बहुत
पहले दोनों खेल रहे थे
लेकिन अब है प्यार बहुत

---

[1] चालाक।

Four Short Verses

A girl with eyes of deepest brown
Is angry with me. What to say?
'But why did we not meet before?'
She fights and says this every day.

We share so many things in love,
But there is just one broken line.
I'm jealous of a friend of hers;
She's jealous of a friend of mine.

We're close, but we stand far away.
There was a secret when we met.
She remembers someone still,
And you—I just cannot forget.

I   was   very   clever   then
And you were very cunning too.
First we thought it was a game.
Now you love me, and I love you.

बेघर

शाम होने को है
लाल सूरज समंदर मे खोने को है
और उसके परे
कुछ परिन्दे
क़तारें बनाए
उन्हीं जंगलों को चले
जिनके पेड़ों की शाखों पे हैं घोंसले
ये परिन्दे
वहीं लौटकर जाएँगे
और सो जाएँगे
हम ही हैरान हैं
इस मकानों के जंगल में
अपना कहीं भी ठिकाना नहीं
शाम होने को है
हम कहाँ जाएँगे

Homeless

The evening draws in,
The red sun begins to hide in the sea.
And over there
Some birds,
Forming a line,
Fly off to those forests,
To those trees, where they have made their nests.
Those birds
Will return to their place
And go to sleep.
Only we are amazed to think
That in this forest of houses
We have no place at all.
The evening draws in.
Where shall we go?